P9-DVJ-353

A GIFT FOR:

FROM:

Bedside Blessings

Charles R. Swindoll

Published by J. Countryman, a division of Thomas Nelson, Inc,
Nashville, Tennessee 37214.

Compiled and edited by Terri Gibbs

Designed by Kirk DouPonce, UDG | DesignWorks, Sisters, Oregon.

ISBN: 0-8499-5740-0

Printed and bound in Belgium

When I remember

You on my bed, I meditate on You

in the night watches.

PSALM 63:6

JANUARY

God's timing
is always on time.

January 1

Mark it down, things do not "just happen." Ours is not a random, whistle-in-the-dark universe. There is a God-arranged plan for this world of ours, which includes a specific plan for you. And through every ordinary day and every extraordinary moment, there is a God who constantly seeks you.

The God who loves us and redeemed us . . . is there, and He is not silent.

Oh the depth of the riches
both of the wisdom and knowledge of God!

Romans 11:33

January 2

God's voice isn't all that difficult to hear. In fact, you almost have to be closing your eyes and stopping your ears to miss it. He sometimes shouts through our pain, whispers to us while we're relaxing on vacation, occasionally He sings to us in a song, and warns us through the sixty-six books of His written Word. It's right there, ink on paper. Count on it—that book will never lead you astray.

I hope in You, O Lord;
You will answer, O Lord my God.

Psalm 38:15

JANUARY 3

Our part. Trust God whole-heartedly, in every corner of life, recognizing that He is the One in charge.

His part. "He will make your paths straight." The word means "smooth," "straight," or "even." In other words, He will smooth out your path. He'll take care of each of those obstacles on the trail ahead of you.

Trust in the LORD
with all your heart. . . . He will
make your paths straight.

PROVERBS 3:5–6

January 4

Serendipity occurs when something beautiful breaks into the monotonous and the mundane. A serendipitous life is marked by "surprisability" and spontaneity. When we lose our capacity for either, we settle into life's ruts. We expect little and we're seldom disappointed.

Though I have walked with God for several decades, I must confess I still find much about Him incomprehensible and mysterious. But this much I know: He delights in surprising us. He dots our pilgrimage from earth to heaven with amazing serendipities.

You open Your hand and
satisfy the desire of every living thing.

Psalm 145:16

January 5

How wonderful that God personally cares about those things that worry us and prey upon our thoughts. He cares about them more than we care about them. Not a single nagging, aching, worrisome, stomach-tensing, blood-pressure-raising thought escapes His notice.

You can throw the whole weight
of your anxieties upon him, for you
are his personal concern.

1 Peter 5:7, Phillips

January 6

Fix your eyes on the Lord! Do it once. Do it daily. Do it ten thousand times ten thousand times. Do it constantly. When your schedule presses, when your prospects thin, when your hope burns low, when people disappoint you, when events turn against you, when dreams die, when the walls close in, when the prognosis seems grim, when your heart breaks, *look at the Lord, and keep on looking at Him.*

Let us fix our eyes on Jesus,
the author and perfecter of our faith.

Hebrews 12:2, NIV

January 7

If I have learned anything during my journey on Planet Earth, it is that people need one another. The presence of other people is essential—caring people, helpful people, interesting people, friendly people, thoughtful people. These folks take the grind out of life. About the time we are tempted to think we can handle things all alone—boom! We run into some obstacle and need assistance. We discover all over again that we are not nearly as self-sufficient as we thought.

A man's counsel
is sweet to his friend.

Proverbs 27:9

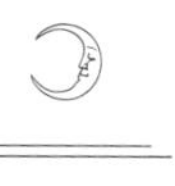

January 8

Be specific in your prayer life. If you need a job, pray for a job. If you're an engineer, ask God to open up an engineering position for you, or something related for which you are qualified. . . . If you need fifteen hundred dollars for tuition, ask or that amount. If some fear has you in its grasp, name that fear and ask specifically for relief from it. . . . "We need," as one of my mentors used to say, "to guard against the slimy ooze of indefiniteness."

Therefore, let everyone
who is godly pray to You.

Psalm 32:6

JANUARY 9

I'd like to deliver a beautiful message to you, my friend. God's hand on your life may be just beginning to make it's mark. That steep hill you've been climbing for such a long time may be the ramp to a destiny beyond your dreams. I do not believe there is any such thing as an accidental or ill-timed birth. You may have arrived in a home that was financially strapped. You may have known brokenness, hurt, and insecurity since your earliest days—but please hear me on this: You were not an accident.

You are a chosen generation,
a royal priesthood, a holy nation,
His own special people.

1 PETER 2:9

January 10

Listen carefully! Jesus Christ opens the gate, gently looks at you, and says: "Come to Me, all you who labor and are . . . over burdened, and I will cause you to rest—I will ease and relieve and refresh your souls" (Matt. 11:28, Amplified).

Nothing complicated. No big fanfare, no trip to Mecca, no hypnotic trance, no fee, no special password. Just come. . . . Unload. . . . His provision is profound, attainable, and right.

You are my hiding place,
You preserve me from trouble

Psalm 32:7

January 11

When was the last time you thanked the Lord for not showing you the future? I'm convinced that one of the best things God does for us is to keep us from knowing what will happen beyond today. Just think of all the stuff you didn't have to worry about just because you never knew it was coming your way!

I trust in You, O LORD, . . .
My times are in Your hand.

PSALM 31:14–15

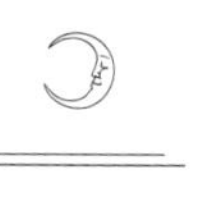

January 12

Our Lord is searching for people who will make a difference. Christians dare not be mediocre. We dare not dissolve into the background or blend into the neutral scenery of this world. Sometimes you have to look awfully close and talk awfully long before an individual will declare his allegiance to God. Sometimes you have to look long and hard to find someone with the courage to stand alone for God. Is that what we have created today in this age of tolerance and compromise?

I searched for a man
among them who would . . .
stand in the gap.

Ezekiel 22:30

January 13

Anybody can accept a reward graciously, and many people can even take their punishment patiently when they have done something wrong. But how many people are equipped to handle mistreatment after they've done right? Only Christians are equipped to do that. That is what makes believers stand out. That's our uniqueness.

Blessed are those who
are persecuted for righteousness' sake,
for theirs is the kingdom of heaven.

Matthew 5:10

January 14

When the X-ray comes back and it doesn't look good, remember, God is still faithful. When you read that heartbreaking note from your mate, remember, God is still faithful. When you hear the worst kind of news about one of your children, remember, God is still faithful. He has not abandoned you, though you're tempted to think He has.

When we are pressed near the heart of God, He is faithful and He will hold us.

In His love . . . He redeemed them,
and He lifted them and carried them.

Isaiah 63:9

January 15

The Word of God doesn't tell us about the truth; it is truth. It doesn't merely contain words about God; it is the Word of God. We don't have to try real had to make it relevant; it is relevant. Don't neglect it. It is the foundation of a stable life. It feeds faith.

The sum of Your word is truth,
and every one of Your righteous
ordinances is everlasting.

Psalm 119:160

January 16

Deceptive baits are set out about us each day, and they don't all come from individuals. Some of them come from a cable television channel or the Internet or a magazine or peer pressure at school or colleagues at work.

So allow me to say this very straight: The greatest gift you can give to your marriage partner is your purity, your fidelity. The greatest character trait you can provide your spouse and your family is moral and ethical self-control. Stand firm my friend. Refuse to yield.

Prove yourselves doers of the word,
and not merely hearers.

James 1:22

January 17

Make no mistake about it, "He's got the whole world in His hands." From the greatest to the least, nothing is beyond the scope of His sovereign power and providential care. He makes the rain fall, the sun shine, the stars twinkle—in this and all other galaxies. He raises up people and kingdoms and He brings down both. He numbers the hairs on our heads and determines the days of our lives. In doing so, He weaves everything together into His design. Ultimately, the tapestry of His handiwork will be something to behold!

Blessed is he
who trusts in the Lord.

Proverbs 16:20

January 18

Whatever form mistreatment takes, it hurts. You feel the horrible rejection. You've done what is right but you've been treated wrongly.

In the midst of all this, remember, God has not abandoned you. He has not forgotten you. He never left. He understands the heartache brought on by the evil He mysteriously permits so He might bring you to a tender, sensitive walk with Him. God is good, Jesus Christ is real—your present circumstances notwithstanding.

I will make them walk
by streams of waters, on a straight path
in which they will not stumble.

Jeremiah 31:9

January 19

Discipline is one of the most hated terms of our times . . . right alongside patience and self-control. But have you noticed how often it comes up in the testimonies of those who win?

No runner completes the training or a race without it.

No human body is kept fit without it.

No temptation is overcome without it.

If you want to put a stop to mediocrity, to replace excuses with fresh determination, . . . you need discipline.

Walk in a manner worthy of the Lord,
to please Him in all respects.

Colossians 1:10

January 20

There have been times in my own life when I've had doubts, when I've stumbled over great cracks that appeared in my world. I've had those times when I climbed into my own bed and wept, crying out to God, just as you have. Such is life, especially when you decide to be real rather than protect some kind of I've-got-it-all-together image. In times like that it's comforting to realize: *God can handle all this.*

The Lord is full of
compassion and is merciful.

James 5:11

January 21

When we look for people to admire, when we choose our role models, our heroes, we are often swayed or impressed by things that are cause for boasting. We want the beautiful people, the brilliant people, the "successful" people. We want the best and the brightest. We are terribly enamored of the surface. The superficial impresses us much more than we'd like to admit.

But God says, "That's not the way I make my choices. I choose the nobodies and turn them into somebodies."

The LORD has sought for Himself
a man after His own heart.

1 Samuel 13:14

January 22

What is God looking for? He is looking for men and women whose hearts are completely His—*completely*. That means there are no locked closets. Nothing's been swept under the rugs. That means that when you do wrong, you admit it and immediately come to terms with it. You're grieved over wrong. You're concerned about those things that displease Him. You long to please Him in your actions. You care about the motivations behind your actions. That's true spirituality.

The eyes of the Lord run to and fro
throughout the whole earth, to show Himself strong on
behalf of those whose heart is loyal to Him.

2 Chronicles 16:9

January 23

If you want to be a person with a large vision, you must cultivate the habit of doing the little things well. That's when God puts iron in your bones! I'm talking about the way you fill out those detailed reports, the way you take care of those daily assignments, or the way you complete the tasks of home or dormitory or work or school. The test of my calling is not how well I do before the public on Sunday; it's how carefully I cover the basis Monday through Saturday when there's nobody to check up on me, when nobody is looking.

He who is faithful in a very
little thing is faithful also in much.

Luke 16:10

January 24

I will hold you up, God says. But as long as you lean on someone else, you can't lean on Me. As long as you lean on some other thing, you won't lean on Me. They become substitutes for Me, so that you aren't being upheld by My hand.

When you lean on another person or another thing, your focus is sideways, not vertical. Human crutches paralyze the walk of faith.

Fear not, for I am with you; . . .
I will uphold you with My righteous
right hand.

Isaiah 41:10

January 25

Discouraged people don't need critics. They hurt enough already. They don't need more guilt or piled-on distress. They need encouragement. In a word, they need a refuge. A place to hide and heal. A willing, caring available someone. A confidant. A comrade at arms. The One called "my Strength . . . my Rock . . . my Fortress." We know Him today by another name: Jesus.

You are my rock and my fortress;
therefore, for Your name's sake,
lead me and guide me.

Psalm 31:3

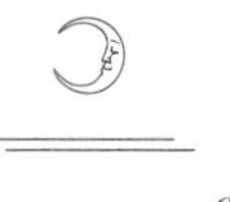

January 26

How often are you to get revenge? "Never," says God. Not usually. Not sometimes. Not occasionally. Not even once!

God says, "so far as it depends on you," be at peace with all. In other words, you can't change the person. All you can do is handle your part, through God's power.

Trust me on this one . . . you'll never regret forgiving someone who doesn't deserve it!

If it is possible,
as much as depends on you,
live peaceably with all men.

Romans 12:18

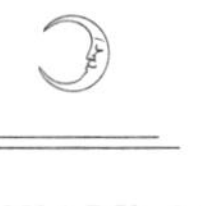

January 27

Perhaps you have known the joys and ecstasies of walking with Christ, but in a moment of despondency you've opted for the wrong fork in the road and you're now in the camp of carnality. . . . But, you've gotten tired of feeling displaced. The disillusionment has bred distrust . . . and the depression is killing you.

Reach up. Come home. The Father is waiting.

God is faithful, through
whom you were called into
fellowship with His son.

1 Corinthians 1:9

JANUARY 28

If your Swiss watch stops working, you don't sit down at home with a screwdriver and start working on it yourself. You take it to a specialist.

The problem is that the Lord gets all the leftovers after we try to fix our problems ourselves. We make all the mistakes and get things tied into granny knots, then dump it in His lap and say, "Here, Lord."

No! Right at first, say, "It's impossible; I can't handle it, Lord. Before I foul it up, it's Yours." He is able to handle it.

Look upon my
affliction and rescue me.

PSALM 119:153

January 29

When God says "no" it is not necessarily discipline or rejection. It may simply be redirection. . . .

The thing we have to do in our walk with God is to listen carefully from day to day. Not just go back to some decision and say, "That's it forever, regardless." We need to look at it each day, keep it fresh, keep the fire hot, keep it on the back burner, saying, "Lord, is this Your arrangement? Is this Your plan? If not, make me sensitive to it. Maybe You're redirecting my life."

Make your ear attentive to wisdom,
incline your heart to understanding.

Proverbs 2:2

January 30

Grace is positive and unconditional acceptance in spite of the other person. Grace is a demonstration of love that is undeserved, unearned, and unrepayable. . . .

That's the way grace is. Grace isn't picky. Grace doesn't look for things that have been done that deserve love. Grace operates apart from the response or the ability of the individual. Grace is one-sided. Grace is God giving Himself in full acceptance to someone who does not deserve it and can never earn it and will never be able to repay.

What does the LORD require of you
but to do justice, to love kindness, and to walk
humbly with your God?

Micah 6:8

January 31

Are times hard? Are days of trouble upon you? When times are tough, the Lord is our only security. The Lord delights in us; He sees and cares about what is happening in our lives, this very moment.

The Lord is our support. In tough times He is our only security. He rescues us because He delights in us. What encouragement that brings.

He brought me out into a broad place;
He delivered me because He delighted in me.

2 Samuel 22:20

FEBRUARY

Every day is that special
day you've been waiting for.
Seize it!

February 1

What is it that drives us on so relentlessly? Are you ready? Take a deep breath and allow yourself to tolerate the one-word answer: PRIDE. We work and push and strive so we can prove we are worthy . . . we are the best . . . we deserve top honors. And the hidden message: I can gain righteousness all on my own, by my own effort, ingenuity, and energy. And because I can, I must! And why is this heretical? Because ultimately this philosophy says: I really don't need divine righteousness.

Pride goes before destruction.

Proverbs 16:18

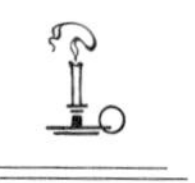

February 2

God has not designed us to live like hermits in a cave. He has designed us to live in friendship and fellowship and community with others. That's why the church, the body of Christ, is so very important, for it is there that we are drawn together in love and mutual encouragement. We're meant to be a part of one another's lives. Otherwise, we pull back, focusing on ourselves—thinking how hard we have it or how unfair others are.

Therefore be imitators of God, . . .
and walk in love.

Ephesians 5:1–2

February 3

The Christian's greatest goal is to be like Christ. We want to emulate His exemplary life, model His method of teaching, resist temptation as He resisted it, handle conflicts as He did, focus on the mission God calls us to accomplish as Christ focused on His. And certainly it is our desire to commune with the Father as the Son did throughout His ministry and suffering. No greater compliment can be given than this one: "When I am with that person, it's like I'm in the presence of Jesus Himself."

We have regard for what is honorable,
not only in the sight of the Lord,
but also in the sight of men.

2 Corinthians 8:21

February 4

To walk by faith does not mean stop *thinking*. To trust God does not imply becoming slovenly or lazy or apathetic. What a distortion of biblical faith. You and I need to trust God for our finances, but that is no license to spend foolishly. You and I ought to trust God for safety in the car, but we're not wise to pass on a blind curve.

Acting foolishly or thoughtlessly, expecting God to bail you out if things go amiss, isn't faith at all. It is *presumption*.

He who comes to God
must believe that He is and that He is
a rewarder of those who seek Him.

Hebrews 11:6

February 5

In all my years of walking with the Lord, I have yet to meet one Christian who has "lived happily ever after." On the other hand, I have met a great many significant saints who have endured affliction, loss, disappointment, setbacks, failures, and incredible pain through the years. And I have seen many of those same men, women . . . cling to their joy, radiate hope, and sustain a winsome spirit . . . even through heartache . . . even through tears . . . even at death's door.

My God shall supply
all your needs according to His riches
in glory in Christ Jesus.

Philippians 4:19

February 6

When we take a tumble and cry out to God in our shame and distress, the psalmist says He "inclines His ear" to us. He bends over to listen. We say, "Oh, Father, I've failed! I've failed terribly. Look at what I've done!" And then He puts His arms around us, just as a loving earthly father would do. He then says, "I accept you just as you are. I acknowledge that what you have done was wrong, as you've confessed it to Me. Now, My son, My daughter, let's move on."

Incline your ear to me,
rescue me quickly; be to me
a rock of strength.

Psalm 31:2

February 7

A healthy fear of God will do much to deter us from sin. When we have a proper fear of the living Lord, we live a cleaner life. Any born-again person who sins willfully has momentarily blocked out his fear of God. You and I can do that. When we actively engage in sin, we consciously put aside what we know to be the truth about God. We suppress the knowledge of Him in our hearts and minds.

By this we know
that we have come to know Him,
if we keep His commandments.

1 John 2:3

February 8

Have you ever noticed how uniquely adapted each animal is to its environment and its way of life? On land, a duck waddles along ungainly on its webbed feet. In the water, it glides along smooth as glass. The rabbit runs with ease and great bursts of speed, but I've never seen one swimming laps. The squirrel climbs anything in sight but cannot fly, while the eagle soars to the mountaintops.

What's true of creatures in the forest is true of Christians in the family. God has not made us all the same. He never intended to.

You are Christ's body,
and individually members of it.

1 Corinthians 12:27

February 9

To be an imitator of God, requires that we come to terms with the value of quietness, slowing down, coming apart from the noise and speed of today's pace, and broadening our lives with a view of the eternal reach of time. It means saying no to more and more activities that increase the speed of our squirrel cage. Knowing God requires that we "be still."

Be still and
know that I am God.

Psalm 46:10, NKJV

February 10

There are four words I wish we would never forget, and they are, "God keeps His word." He doesn't tell us one thing and then do another. He doesn't, as we say, string us along. God doesn't lead us to believe something and then leave us in the lurch and let us down. God has veracity. He operates in one realm, and that is the realm of truth. You can trust Him.

The Lord is good to all,
and His mercies are over all His works.

Psalm 145:9

FEBRUARY 11

What does it mean to be a person after God's own heart? Seems to me, it means that you are a person whose life is in harmony with the Lord. What is important to Him is important to you. What burdens Him burdens you. When He says, "Go to the right," you go to the right. When He says, "Stop that in your life," you stop it. When He says, "This is wrong and I want you to change," you come to terms with it because you have a heart for God. That's bottom-line biblical Christianity.

Applying all diligence,
in your faith supply moral excellence.

2 PETER 1:5

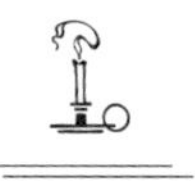

February 12

We have to deal with attitudes as severely as we deal with actions. Christian parents, learn that! Come down hard on wrong attitudes! But when you catch those beautiful glimpses of right attitudes, reward! Build up! Of course, in order to do that, and to be a consistent role model, your own attitudes must be right.

The reward of humility and the
fear of the LORD *are riches, honor, and life.*

Proverbs 22:4

February 13

Someone once asked Mother Teresa what the job description was for anyone who might wish to work alongside her in the grimy streets and narrow alleys of Calcutta. Without hesitation she mentioned only two things: the desire to work hard and a joyful attitude. It has been my observation that both of those qualities are rare. But the second is much rarer than the first. Diligence may be difficult to find, but compared to an attitude of genuine joy, hard work is commonplace.

O clap your hands, all peoples;
shout to God with the voice of joy.

Psalm 47:1

February 14

Harmonious partnerships are the result of hard work; they never "just happen." I don't know of anything that helps this process more than deep, honest, regular communication. . . . That's not just talking; it's also listening. And not just listening, but also hearing. Not just hearing, but also responding, calmly and kindly.

The "hard work" also includes giving just as much as taking, . . . forgiving as quickly as confronting, putting into the marriage more than you ever expect out of it. In one word it means being *unselfish*.

Love . . . does not seek its own,
is not provoked.

1 Corinthians 13:4–5

February 15

Whenever the New Testament lingers on the subject of sensual temptation, it gives us one command: RUN! The Bible does not tell us to reason with it. It does not tell us to think about it and claim verses. It tells us to FLEE! I have discovered you cannot yield to sensuality of you're running away from it. So? Run for your life! Get out of there! If you try to reason with lust or play around with sensual thoughts, you will finally yield. You can't fight it. That's why the Spirit of God forcefully commands, "Run!"

God is faithful, who will not allow you
to be tempted beyond what you are able, but with
the temptation will provide the way of escape.

1 Corinthians 10:13

February 16

I have discovered that a joyful countenance has nothing to do with one's age or one's occupation (or lack of it) or one's geography or education or marital status or good looks or circumstances. Joy is a choice. It is a matter of attitude that stems from one's confidence in God—that He is at work, that He is in full control, that He is in the midst of whatever has happened, is happening, and will happen.

You will make me to know the path of life;
in Your presence is fullness of joy.

Psalm 16:11

February 17

On each occasion when we observe the Lord's Table, let us give thanks that our Savior gave thanks for us and that He was compelled by love to take up that cross. As we hold that cup close to our lips, in remembrance, may we taste and see that the Lord is good. Think of the significance of that. We are not simply to feel or to read or to hear or to see, but to take into our very bodies the taste of our Savior's sacrifice.

O taste and see that the
Lord is good; how blessed is the man
who takes refuge in Him!

Psalm 34:8

February 18

Our human ways are based on what seems fair. We firmly believe that when someone does what is right, rewards and blessings result. When someone does what is wrong, there are serious consequences, even punishment. But that's our way, not necessarily God's way. At least not immediately. He's been known to allow unfair treatment to occur in the lives of some absolutely innocent folks—for reasons far more profound and deep than they or we could have imagined.

I do all things for the sake of the gospel,
so that I may become a fellow partaker of it.

1 Corinthians 9:23

FEBRUARY 19

Without exception, people who consistently laugh do so in spite of, seldom because of anything. They pursue fun rather than wait for it to knock on their door in the middle of the day. Such infectiously joyful believers have no trouble convincing people around them that Christianity is real and that Christ can transform a life. Joy is the flag that flies above the castle of their hearts, announcing that the King is in residence.

Rejoice in the LORD always;
again I will say, rejoice!

PHILIPPIANS 4:4

February 20

Perhaps you are in the crucible of decision—a time of deep, searching struggle in your soul. God has made it fairly clear to you that this is what He wants of you, and this is His will for your life. But it involves giving up certain rights that you enjoy, certain desires that are significant and important to you. Letting God have His way can be an uncomfortable thing.

I, even I, am He
who comforts you. Who are you that
you are afraid of man. . . .?

Isaiah 51:12

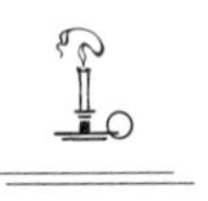

February 21

Having a contagious, positive attitude toward God does not mean living unrealistically where you tell everybody nice, upbeat things all the time, whether they are true or not. I believe in thinking positively, but I don't believe in phony baloney. I believe in thinking positively, because I believe that's the only way Christians really think aright, as we see things through Christ's eyes. But that's not the same as thinking unrealistically or living in a dream world or saying something to someone just to make them feel good.

The Lord is a refuge for
His people and a stronghold.

Joel 3:16

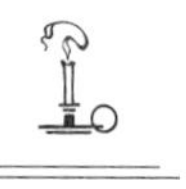

February 22

You want a fresh burst of encouragement? You may have a good friend who is not walking as close to the Lord as he or she once was. Here is fresh hope. Rest in the confidence that God has neither lost interest nor lost control. The Lord has not folded His arms and looked the other way. That person you are concerned about may be your son or daughter. Find encouragement in this firm confidence: The One who began a good work in your boy or in your girl will bring it to completion; He will finish the task.

He who began a good work in you
will perfect it until the day of Christ Jesus.

Philippians 1:6

February 23

Jesus of Nazareth, had a magnificent obsession: the cross. Painful and anguishing though it was, He found Himself consumed by a compelling sense of Divine providence, and each day of His adult life drew Him inexorably closer to the fulfillment of His mission.

Jesus was not a helpless victim of fate; He was not a pitiful martyr. . . . His death on the cross was no afterthought on God's part but rather, the fulfillment of the Father's predetermined plan for His Son.

It is written, that the Christ would suffer
and rise again from the dead the third day,
and that repentance for forgiveness of sins
would be proclaimed in His name.

Luke 24:46–47

February 24

The cause of disillusionment is putting one's complete hope and trust in people. Putting people on a pedestal, focusing on them, finding our security in them. Being so horizontally locked in that the person takes the place of God, even becomes God. Your complete hope can rest in one person. It can be your child. It can be your parent. It can be a business partner, a friend, a pastor, a coach, a mate. And when the feet of clay crumble (as surely they will), total disillusionment sets in.

What's the cure? Putting our complete hope and trust in the living Lord.

You are my hope;
O Lord God, You are my confidence.

Psalm 71:5

FEBRUARY 25

In its earliest form the word *peace* meant "to bind together" and came to include the whole idea of being bound so closely together with something or someone that a harmony resulted. The right woman who is joined in harmony with the right man in marriage begins a "peaceful" companionship. One friend who is joined in heart and soul to another friend sustains a "peaceful" relationship where harmony exists. When there is such grace-and-peace harmony, choosing joy flows naturally.

Grace to you and peace from God
our Father and the Lord Jesus Christ.

PHILIPPIANS 1:2

February 26

The entire sweep of history hinges on a tiny window of time in the first century, and through that window we see a cross. All of history looks back at that moment—to the tragedy and triumph of that cross. First the crucifixion, then the resurrection of the Son of God. Those two epochal events secure our eternal destiny.

God demonstrates
His own love toward us, in that while we
were yet sinners, Christ died for us.

Romans 5:8

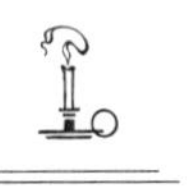

February 27

All whom God uses greatly are first hidden in the secret of His presence, away from the pride of man. It is there our vision clears. It is there the silt drops from the current of our life and our faith begins to grasp His arm. Abraham waited for the birth of Isaac. Moses didn't lead the Exodus until he was eighty. Elijah waited beside the brook. Noah waited 120 years for rain. Paul was hidden away for three years in Arabia. God is working while His people are waiting, waiting, waiting.

That's what's happening. For the present time, nothing. For the future, everything!

Wait for the Lord; be strong and let
your heart take courage; yes, wait for the Lord.

Psalm 27:14

February 28

When money is our objective, we must live in fear of losing it, which makes us paranoid and suspicious. When fame is our aim, we become competitive lest others upstage us, which makes us envious. When power and influence drive us, we become self-serving and strong-willed, which makes us arrogant. . . . All these pursuits fly in the face of contentment . . . and joy.

Only Christ can satisfy, whether we have or don't have, whether we are known or unknown, whether we live or die.

To me, to live is Christ and to die is gain.

Philippians 1:21

MARCH

God has
called us to be Holy.
So let's be holy.

MARCH 1

Anyone can love the lovely. Anyone can forgive the forgivable. But Christians are unique. We are called to love the unlovely, to forgive the unforgivable. Jesus' followers have done so for centuries.

Few acts have a greater impact on those who mistreat us and abuse us than our telling them we forgive them, and we are asking God to forgive them too.

Keep fervent in your
love for one another, because love
covers a multitude of sins.

1 PETER 4:8

March 2

God can use our authority and our abundance and our promotion. But before He can, we need to humble ourselves before God's mighty hand and say, "Jesus Christ, I need You. I have all of this to account for, and I can't take any of it with me. Please use me as you see fit." With authority comes the need for accountability. With popularity comes the need for humility. With prosperity comes the need for integrity.

Humble yourselves
in the presence of the Lord,
and He will exalt you.

James 4:10

March 3

When we arrive at dilemmas in life and are unable to decipher the right direction to go, if we hope to maintain our joy in the process, we must (repeat must) allow the Lord to be our Guide, our Strength, our Wisdom—our all!

If you are the super-responsible, I-can-handle-it individual who tends to be intense and impatient, letting go and letting God take charge will be one of life's most incredible challenges. But I urge you, do it! Force yourself to trust Another who is far more capable and intelligent and responsible than you.

Our God forever and ever; . . .
will guide us until death.

Psalm 48:14

March 4

Grace is extended even to those who fail.

Have you failed in some area of your life? Have you been disobedient?

The grace of God is provided for those who fail, for those of us who are sinners. The solution is found in coming back. He will forgive and reinstate you. If it were not so, we would all despair.

Return to the LORD your God,
for He is gracious and compassionate, . . .
abounding in lovingkindness.

JOEL 2:13

March 5

The message of Jesus Christ cuts across all strata of status and success. It doesn't make any difference what your salary or lifestyle is, what car you drive, where you live, or where you work. None of those factors have a lot to do with your position before God.

Whoever believes that
Jesus is the Christ is born of God.

1 John 5:1

March 6

A number of years ago, somebody counted the promises in the Bible and totaled up 7,474. I can't verify that number, but I do know that within the pages of the Bible there are thousands of promises that grab the reader and say, "Believe me! Accept me! Hold on to me!" And of all the promises in the Bible, the ones that often mean the most are the promises that offer hope at the end of affliction. Those promises that tell us, "It's worth it. Walk with Me. Trust Me. Wait with Me. I will reward you."

As for me, I trust in You,
O Lord, I say, "You are my God."

Psalm 31:14

March 7

The Scripture teaches that even though Jesus did become a man, He never was anything less than God. Yet for a period of thirty-three earthly years He voluntarily gave up the independent exercise of His own rights as God. While on earth He submitted Himself to the Father, so that every word was spoken as God would have Him speak it, and every act was done precisely as God would have Him do it.

I do not seek My own will,
but the will of Him who sent Me.

John 5:30

March 8

I have never seen a habit just lie down, surrender, and die; we have to make a conscious effort if we hope to break longstanding habits. If you are negative today, chances are very good that when you wake up tomorrow morning you're still going to be negative. In fact, you'll be even better at it tomorrow morning because you'll have perfected it for one more day. So force a vertical focus. That means first, you pray for strength. Then you make a conscious effort to respond.

Walk in a manner worthy
of the God who calls you into His
own kingdom and glory.

1 Thessalonians 2:12

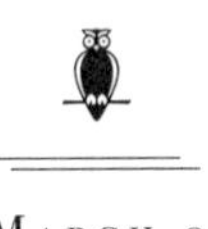

March 9

Everything that was involved in Jesus' becoming human began with an attitude of submission . . . a willingness to cooperate with God's plan for salvation. Rather than lobbying for His right to remain in heaven and continuing to enjoy all the benefits of that exalted role as the second member of the Godhead and Lord of the created world, He willingly said yes. He agreed to cooperate with a plan that would require His releasing ecstasy and accepting agony.

I have come down from heaven,
not to do My own will, but the will
of Him who sent me.

John 6:38

MARCH 10

Being unselfish in attitude strikes at the very core of our being. It means we are willing to forego our own comfort, our own preferences, our own schedule, or own desires for another's benefit. And that brings us back to Christ. Perhaps you never realized that it was His attitude of unselfishness that launched Him from the splendor of heaven to a humble manger in Bethlehem . . . and later to the cross at Calvary. How did He accept all that? Willingly.

Little children,
let us not love with word or with tongue,
but in deed and truth.

1 JOHN 3:18

March 11

Stay open to a new idea for at least five minutes. Don't try it for an entire day, because you'll almost panic. Just take on your day five minutes at a time. When something new, something unexpected, confronts you, don't respond with an immediate "Nope! Never!" Wait five minutes. Hold off. Tolerate the possibility for five minutes. You could be surprised at the benefit of remaining open those three hundred seconds.

Behold, I will do something new,
now it will spring forth;
will you not be aware of it?

Isaiah 43:19

March 12

Having been swamped by sin all our lives, struggling to find our way to the top of the water to breathe, we can find great hope in the ability God gives us not only to breathe but to swim freely. You see, Christ not only lived an exemplary life, He also makes it possible for us to do the same. He gives us His pattern to follow *without* while at the same time providing the needed power *within*.

Since He Himself was tempted, . . .
He is able to come to the aid of those
who are tempted.

Hebrews 2:18

March 13

Attitude is so crucial in the life of the Christian. We can go through the Sunday motions, we can carry out the religious exercises, we can pack a Bible under our arms, and sing the songs from memory, yet we can still hold grudges against the people who have wronged us. In our own way—and it may even be with a little religious manipulation—we'll get back at them. But that is not God's way.

Love . . . does not take
into account a wrong suffered.

1 Corinthians 13:4–5

March 14

Spiritually speaking, the ultimate purpose of our lives is "His good pleasure." Our lives are to be lived for God's greater glory—not our own selfish desires.

Are we left to do so all alone? Is it our task to gut it out, grit our teeth, and do His will? Not at all. Here's the balance: God is at work in us! He is the one who gives us strength and empowers our diligence. As He pours His power into us, we do the things that bring Him pleasure. Take special note that His pleasure (not ours), His will (not ours), His glory (not ours) are what make life meaningful.

We should be holy and without blame before Him in love . . . according to the good pleasure of His will.

Ephesians 1:4–5

March 15

Inevitably, spring follows winter. Every year. Yes, including this one. Barren days, like naked limbs, will soon be clothed with fresh life. Do you need that reminder today? Are you ready for some sunshine on your shoulders . . . a few green sprouts poking up through all that white? A light at the end of your tunnel?

Look! There it is in the distance. It may be tiny, but it's there.

Your light will break out like
the dawn, and your recovery will
speedily spring forth.

Isaiah 58:8

March 16

When I'm able, by faith, to sense God's hand in my situation, my attitude will be right. I don't begin the day gritting my teeth, asking, "Why do I have to stay in this situation?" Instead, I believe that He made me the way I am and put me where I am to do what He has planned for me to do. I don't wait for my situation to change before I put my heart into my work. I suggest you give that a try. It's called "blooming where you are planted." There's nothing like an attitude of gratitude to free us up.

Seek the Lord and His strength; . . .
remember His wonders which He has done.

Psalm 105:4–5

March 17

When our world begins to get too serious, we need momentary interruptions of just plain fun. A surprising day off, a long walk in the woods, a movie, an enjoyable evening relaxing with a friend over a bowl of popcorn, a game of racquetball or golf—these diversions can make all the difference in our ability to cope with life's crushing demands. We need to give ourselves permission to enjoy various moments in life even though all of life is not in perfect order. This takes practice, but it's worth the effort.

Our mouth was filled with laughter
and our tongue with joyful shouting.

Psalm 126:2

March 18

Jesus was the first to teach us that each one of us has a cross to bear. We may not necessarily look as if we are bearing one, but we are. Each of us has some area of pain and suffering in life. The world around us would have us run from that burden—to resent it, hate it. Instead, we should—and I know this is tough to hear and believe—embrace it.

He who does not take
his cross and follow after Me is
not worthy of Me.

Matthew 10:38

MARCH 19

Too often the fog of the flesh blocks out our ability to see God's plan. Our selfishness pushes away His hand because we want our way. Our location and our situation become irksome assignments, and life becomes barren and cold.

The only way to find happiness in the grind of life is to do so by faith. A faith-filled life means all the difference in how we view everything around us. It affects our attitudes toward people, toward location, toward situation, toward circumstances, toward ourselves. Only then do our feet become swift to do what is right.

Being always of good courage . . .
we walk by faith, not by sight.

2 CORINTHIANS 5:6–7

March 20

There is something wonderfully exciting about reaching into the future with excited anticipation, and those who pursue new adventures through life stay younger, think better, and laugh louder! I just spoke with a middle-aged man who told me he hopes to teach himself Mandarin, one of the Chinese dialects, so that when he takes an early retirement in a few years he can go to China and teach English as a second language. He was smiling from ear to ear.

I know the plans
that I have for you, . . . to give you
a future and a hope.

Jeremiah 29:11

March 21

Calamities aren't from "Mother Nature." Take those superficial words out of your vocabulary. Understand that God, in His sovereignty, places His hand over our lives and allows us to pass through painful experiences that we would never choose or want. Yet when we go through them, accepting them and learning from them, we grow deeper in the Christian life. In the final analysis, if we've responded correctly, we become more obedient.

Everything God does will
remain forever; there is nothing to add to it
and there is nothing to take from it.

Ecclesiates 3:14

MARCH 22

May I confess something to you? I don't think I have ever learned any deep, lasting, life-changing lessons on the crest of success. I have learned very little from winning, but I have learned a great deal from losing. For that is when I pull off my rose-colored glasses, put on my realism spectacles, and say "This kind of thing could come only from God. I'd better sit up and take notice."

Teach me Your way,
O LORD; I will walk in Your truth.

PSALM 86:11

March 23

Christ came back from the dead so we might live as He lived and claim the triumph He has provided. He didn't die just to be studied and oohhed and aahhed over; He died and rose again to offer, through His blood and His life, new life—transforming power to live beyond the dregs of depravity's leftovers.

I came that they
may have life, and have
it abundantly.

John 10:10

March 24

Making a major move can be one of the most insecure times we ever face in life. Pulling up roots in one place and trying to put them down in another can be not only fearful but depressing. For the Christian this is heightened by a sense of wonder over whether God is in the move. . . . I'm referring not only to a geographical move but also to a career change or a domestic move from single to married. Big, big changes! The assurance that God is with us during such alterations in lifestyle and adjustment periods is terribly important.

Let endurance have
its perfect result, so that you may be perfect
and complete, lacking nothing.

James 1:4

March 25

Trials and tests come that impact our patience and give it a chance to grow (do they ever!). As patience begins to develop, strong character is cultivated, moving us ever onward toward maturity. There is no shortcut! But by refusing to squirm out of your problems, you find yourself becoming the man or woman you have always wanted to be.

When the way is rough,
your patience has a chance to grow.

James 1:2-4, TLB

March 26

The Christian is a weird sort, let's face it. We are earthlings, yet the Bible says we are citizens of heaven. This world may not be our home, but it is our residence. Furthermore, we are to live in the world, but we are not to be of the world. And since joy is one of our distinctives, laughter is appropriate even though we are surrounded by all manner of wrong and wickedness. It can get a little confusing.

Our citizenship is in heaven,
from which also we eagerly wait for a Savior,
the Lord Jesus Christ.

Philippians 3:20

March 27

Settle it in your mind once for all: Christians are not supernaturally protected from the blasts, the horrors, the aches, or the pains of living on this globe. Christians can be unfairly treated, assaulted, robbed, raped, and murdered. We can suffer financial reversals, we can be taken advantage of, abused, neglected, and divorced by uncaring mates. Then how can we expect to be joyful, unlike those around us? Because God promises that deep within He will give us peace . . . an unexplainable, illogical inner peace.

In the world you have tribulation,
but take courage; I have overcome the world.

John 16:33

March 28

In Christ, through His death and resurrection, there is life with God throughout eternity.

We stake our lives not on nursery rhymes or human-viewpoint philosophies, but on His death and resurrection. Rather than trying hard to grope our way through the maze of manmade ideas and opinions, through Christ we find ourselves empowered by the tragedy and triumph of the cross.

While we were enemies
we were reconciled to God through
the death of His Son.

Romans 5:10

March 29

No one, no matter how successful in this life, can claim victory over death all on his or her own. We may climb our ladders of achievement, of higher education, of financial prosperity, of athletic reputation, of faithful and diligent responsibility, of integrity in business, of high moral standards. But only through faith in Christ do we have the assurance of hope beyond the grave.

If we have died
with Christ, we believe that we
shall also live with Him.

Romans 6:8

March 30

It is not our behavior on Sunday morning that demonstrates the depth of our Christian faith to the world. It's the way we behave at our work, on the job. You ask a person who works alongside you or under you or over you or on the same team about your Christianity and that person will not talk about your life on Sunday. That person will talk about what you are like to work with or to work for, day after day after day, all week long.

The fear of the Lord
is the beginning of wisdom.

Proverbs 9:10

March 31

Leadership calls for the stretching of creativity. If you are a leader, you will occasionally find yourself up against a blank wall. It's big and intimidating and usually tall and slick. You can't push through it, climb over it, or see your way around it. That's when it gets exciting! That's when innovative juices start to flow and you begin to think about possible ways to get beyond that wall. Innovation and creativity (not to mention courage) team up, determined to find an answer and a way.

The plans of the diligent
lead surely to advantage.

Proverbs 21:5

APRIL

Every journey
is accomplished one
step at a time.

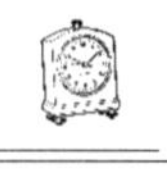

April 1

Integrity keeps your eyes on your own paper during the test. Integrity makes you record and submit only true figures on your expense account. Integrity keeps your personal life pure and straight, regardless of the benefits and personal perks that might come your way through compromise.

Make no mistake, integrity is tough stuff. Integrity does not take the easy way, make the easy choices, or choose the "pleasures for a season" path. Integrity is what you are when there isn't anyone around to check up on you.

A good name is to be
more desired than great wealth.

Proverbs 22:1

April 2

The non-Christian world may be lost and running on empty, but they are not stupid or unaware of their surroundings. When they come across an individual who is at peace, free of fear and worry, fulfilled, and genuinely happy, no one has to tell them that something is missing from their lives. Ours may be a mad, bad, sad world, but it is not blind. And it is certainly not unreachable.

You yourself are a guide
to the blind, a light to those
who are in darkness.

Romans 2:19

April 3

Someday we will stand before God. And when we do, we will need something more than speculative imagination or a warm, fuzzy feeling about nature. When we pass from time into the presence of the Eternal God, we will need more than good medical assistance or the promise of some well-meaning friend. We will need a living Redeemer, whose nail-pierced hands hold our salvation.

Christ redeemed us from the curse
of the Law, having become a curse for us.

Galatians 3:13

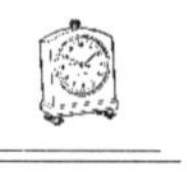

April 4

Even as we rest in what God has done on our behalf, let us be on the tiptoe of expectancy—working, serving, giving, loving, keeping the faith and demonstrating that faith to the world of men and women around us. And dedicating ourselves in loving service to God and humanity.

I have no greater joy
than this, to hear of my children
walking in the truth.

3 John 1:4

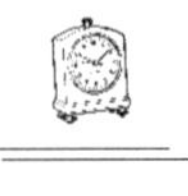

April 5

On the cross, the Lord God arranged a plan for our spiritual survival with divine integrity. It required the sacrifice of Christ on the cross. He followed through. We can take Him at His word. He was who He said He was, and He did what He said He would do. With a single heart and a single mind and a single will, He fulfilled the Father's plan.

Let us hold fast the confession
of our hope without wavering, for He
who promised is faithful.

Hebrews 10:23

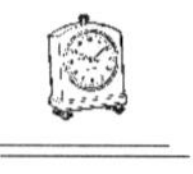

April 6

God deals with the hard questions of life. Not questions like how do I make a living, but how do I make a life? Not how do I spend my time, but how do I spend eternity? And not so much how do I get along with the person who sits next to me, but ultimately, how do I get along with God? When we answer the hard questions correctly, all the others fall into place.

Godliness actually is a means
of great gain when accompanied
by contentment.

1 Timothy 6:6

April 7

Our earthly culture is pagan to the core. Let's not forget that God has left us here on purpose. We're here to demonstrate what it is like to be a member of another country, to have a citizenship in another land, so that we might create a desire for others to emigrate. Our mission is to create a thirst and an interest in that land "beyond the blue."

I will also make You a light of
the nations so that My salvation may
reach to the end of the earth..

Isaiah 49:6

April 8

Our citizenship is in heaven." But let's never forget that our involvement is on earth. That may create a little tension now and then, but what a challenging opportunity! Only heaven-bound people are objective enough to make a major difference on earth. While we "eagerly wait for a Savior," we are able to introduce earth-bound people to a whole new way of life.

Our citizenship is in heaven,
from which also we eagerly
wait for a Savior.

Philippians 3:20

April 9

Are you aware of the joy-stealing effect an unforgiving spirit is having on your life?

Start by telling God how much it hurts and that you need Him to help you to forgive the offense. Get rid of all the poison of built-up anger and pour out all the acid of long-term resentment. Fully forgive the offender. Once that is done, you will discover that you no longer rehearse the ugly scenes in your mind. The revengeful desire to get back and get even will wane, and in its now-empty space will come a new spirit of joy.

Walk in a manner worthy of
the calling with which you have been called,
with all humility and gentleness.

Ephesians 4:1–2

April 10

By making us in His image, God gave us capacities not given to other forms of life. Ideally, He made us to know Him, to love Him, and to obey Him. He did not put rings in our noses that He might pull us around like oxen, nor did He create us with strings permanently attached to our hands and feet like human marionettes to control and manipulate our every move. What pleasure would He have in the love of a puppet or the obedience of a dumb animal?

No, He gave us freedom to make choices.

Choose life in
order that you may live.

Deuteronomy 30:19

April 11

Solomon writes that "a cheerful heart has a continual feast" and he is right. I find that a spirit of cheer spreads rapidly. Before you know it, others have joined you at the table. Choose joy! There are very few days in my life during which I find nothing to laugh at. Laughter is the most familiar sound in the hallway where my staff and I work alongside each other. And what a contagious thing is outrageous joy . . . everybody wants to be around it. So, rejoice!

A cheerful heart
has a continual feast.

Proverbs 15:15

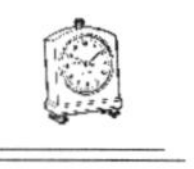

April 12

Instead of living in the grip of fear, held captive by the chains of tension and dread, when we release our preoccupation with worry, we find God's hand at work on our behalf. He, our "God of peace," comes to our aid, changing people, relieving tension, altering difficult circumstances. The more you practice giving your mental burdens to the Lord, the more exciting it gets to see how God will handle the things that are impossible for you to do anything about.

He Himself is our peace.

Ephesians 2:14

April 13

God's goal is that we move toward maturity—all our past failures and faults and hang-ups notwithstanding.

God's specialty is bringing renewal to our strength, not reminders of our weakness. Take it by faith. He is well aware of your weaknesses; He just sovereignly chooses not to stop there. They become the platform upon which He does His best work. Cheer up! There is great hope.

My son, do not forget my teaching,
but let your heart keep my commandments.

Proverbs 3:1

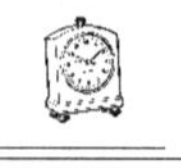

April 14

Since our citizenship is in heaven, planet Earth is really not our home. For us, it is foreign soil. We are citizens of another realm. We belong to the kingdom of God. Consequently, we need to be on our best behavior; otherwise, people will get a distorted perception of what our homeland is like. As a result of our behavior, they will either be attracted to or repelled by heaven, the place we call home.

By this all men will know
that you are My disciples, if you have
love for one another.

John 13:35

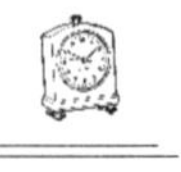

April 15

Nothing speaks louder or more powerfully than a life of integrity. Absolutely nothing! Nothing stands the test like solid character. You can handle the blast like a steer in a blizzard. The ice may form on your horns, but you keep standing against the wind and the howling, raging storm because Christ is at work in your spirit. Character will always win the day. As Horace Greeley wrote: "Fame is a vapor, popularity an accident, riches take wing, and only character endures."

Those who love Your law
have great peace, and nothing causes
them to stumble.

Psalm 119:165

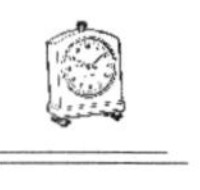

April 16

We appreciate what people do. We affirm who they are. When we say thank you to someone who completes a task, we are expressing our appreciation. But when we acknowledge and express our gratitude for what others are—in character, in motive, in heart—we are affirming them personally. A mark of maturity is the ability to affirm, not just appreciate.

Wisdom is in
the presence of the one who
has understanding.

Proverbs 17:24

April 17

Some people are thermometers. They merely register what is around them. If the situation is tight and pressurized, they register tension and irritability. If it's stormy, they register worry and fear. If it's calm, quiet, and comfortable, they register relaxation and peacefulness.

Others, however, are thermostats. They regulate the atmosphere. They are the mature change-agents who never let the situation dictate to them.

I have learned to be content
in whatever circumstances I am.

Philippians 4:11

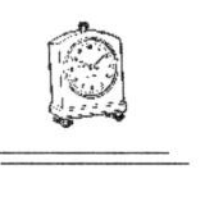

April 18

Because the Christian has the Lord Himself dwelling within, the potential for inner strength (i.e. confidence) is unlimited. This explains why those who gave their lives for whatever righteous cause down through the ages did so with such courage. Often they were physically weak individuals, small in stature, but they refused to back down. Only the indwelling, empowering Christ can give someone that much confidence.

He has satisfied the thirsty soul,
and the hungry soul He has filled
with what is good.

Psalm 107:9

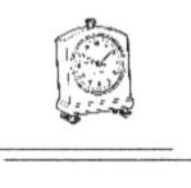

April 19

Heaven is something we inherit. We are undeserving, therefore we do not *earn* heaven; it is a *gift* provided by the One who went before us. "It is the kingdom prepared for you."

Since the beginning of time, God has anticipated the joy of His people in His presence throughout eternity.

Your kingdom is
an everlasting kingdom,
and Your dominion endures
throughout all generations.

Psalm 145:13

April 20

God's sense of humor has intrigued me for years. What amazes me, however, is the number of people who don't think He has one. For the life of me, I can't figure out why they can't see it. He made you and me, didn't He? And what about all those funny-looking creatures that keep drawing us back to the zoo? If they aren't proof of our Creator's sense of humor, I don't know what is.

Surely it is not blasphemous to think that laughter breaks out in heaven on special occasions. Why shouldn't it?

Let the godly ones exult in glory;
let them sing for joy.

Psalm 149:5

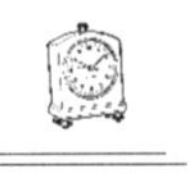

April 21

We need to learn the deep and enduring value of the hidden life.

When I think of hidden lives, I think of mothers of small children. I think of compassionate men and women who are now caring for elderly parents. I think of highly capable or qualified individuals, who, it seems, for the time being, are completely useless. I think of students still in the classroom, preparing, preparing, preparing. It's the hidden life—the life where lasting lessons are learned.

God is not unjust so as to
forget your work and the love which you
have shown toward His name.

Hebrews 6:10

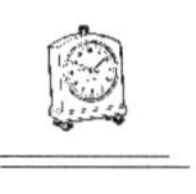

April 22

To make this thing called life work, we gotta lean and support. And relate and respond. And give and take. And confess and forgive. And reach out and embrace. And release and rely.

Especially in God's family . . . where working together is Plan A for survival. And since we're each so different (thanks to the way God built us), love and acceptance are not optional luxuries. Neither is tolerance. Or understanding. Or patience. You know, all those things you need from others when your humanity crowds out your divinity.

Whoever loves the Father
loves the child born of Him.

1 John 5:1

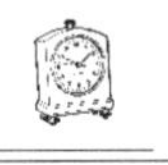

April 23

Nothing makes us more uncertain and insecure than not being sure we are in the will of God. And nothing is more encouraging than knowing for sure that we are. Then, no matter what the circumstances, no matter what happens, we can stand fast.

We can be out of a job but know that we are in the will of God. We can face a threatening situation but know that we are in the will of God. We can have the odds stacked against us but know that we are in the will of God. Nothing intimidates those who know that what they believe is based on what God has said.

The one who does
the will of God lives forever.

1 John 2:17

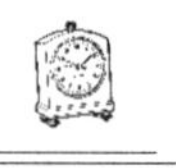

April 24

Christians are not living on this earth as carefree tourists. We are not vacationing our way to heaven. We are soldiers on raw, pagan soil. Everywhere around us the battle rages. The danger is real, and the enemy is formidable. Christ died not only to gain victory over sin's dominion but to equip us for that fight—to give us the inner strength we need to stand against it. Therefore . . . we are to arm ourselves with the strength that Christ gives because our purpose in life is the same as His.

Beloved, I urge you as
aliens and strangers to abstain from fleshly
lusts which wage war against the soul.

1 Peter 2:11

April 25

Many of you live in the competitive jungle of the business world, and some of you may work for a boss who asks you to compromise your ethics and integrity. Pressured by the tension between pleasing your boss, who can fire you or demote you or just make your life difficult, and your commitment to Christ, you need the inner resources to stand firm. The good news is this: you have it! The provision Christ gives will be sufficient for such a stress test.

You have need of endurance,
so that when you have done the will of God,
you may receive what was promised.

Hebrews 10:36

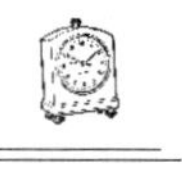

April 26

I have never met a person who didn't have a reason to blame someone else. Every one of us can blame somebody for something that has happened in our lives. But don't waste your time. What we need most is a steady stream of love flowing among us. Love that quickly forgives and willingly overlooks and refuses to take offense.

Beloved, if God
so loved us, we also ought
to love one another.

1 John 4:11

April 27

God is in sovereign control. In the midst of those very circumstances that today have you baffled, wondering what you're going to do, or even how you're going to go on, you can rest assured that God's power and sovereign control are already at work. God never knows frustration. He never has to scratch His head, wondering what in the world He's going to do next with people like us, or with the nations of this world.

O God, You are
awesome from Your sanctuary.

Psalm 68:35

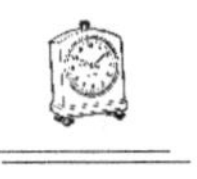

April 28

God's presence is not as intriguing as His absence. His voice is not as eloquent as His silence. Who of us has not longed for a word from God, searched for a glimpse of His power, or yearned for the reassurance of His presence, only to feel that He seems absent from the moment? Distant. Preoccupied. Maybe even unconcerned. Yet later, we realize how very present He was all along.

The LORD is my shepherd,
I shall not want. . . . He guides me in
the paths of righteousness.

Psalm 23: 1, 3

April 29

Theologians have spent lifetimes searching out the traits, the characteristics, the hand of God in Scripture. Yet, those who are truly honest and humble enough to admit the truth come to the end of their earthly lives acknowledging that they have barely scratched the surface.

As the heavens
are higher than the earth, so are . . .
my thoughts than your thoughts.

Isaiah 55:9

April 30

God knows where we are. Sometimes we forget this. Sometimes we even feel that God has forgotten us. He hasn't. God knows exactly where we are. So when you are afflicted with those forsaken feelings, when you're on the verge of throwing a pity party thanks to those despairing thoughts, go back to the Word of God.

Do not fear,
for I am with you.

Isaiah 41:10:

MAY

God's mercies
are new every morning.

May 1

Pride, fear, resentment, and habit are all tough evidences of the flesh. But those who are being shaped into the image of Christ do not go the way of the flesh. Women and men of God do not manipulate events so that they can be pleased and get what they want. That's why God crushes pride, removes fear, breaks into resentment, and changes long-standing habits until the whole inner being is renovated . . . until we rest in our God and are ready for His will, not ours, to be done.

Discipline yourself
for the purpose of godliness.

1 Timothy 4:7

May 2

When we keep God's glory uppermost in our minds, it's amazing how much else falls into place. Since He gets the glory, we're more comfortable leaving the results with Him in His time. Since He gets the glory, our umbrella of love expands to cover others. Since He gets the glory, it's easier for us to show hospitality to others, for we're ultimately serving Him. Since He gets the glory, exercising our gifts is not a pain but a privilege. The benefits are endless when the glory goes to God!

Yours is the kingdom
and the power and the glory forever.

Matthew 6:13

May 3

No matter what its source or intensity, there's something about suffering that simplifies life and draws us back to the basics. Invariably, especially during a time of intense trial, I go back to my theological roots. I go back to what I really believe. I return to the essentials such as prayer and dependence, like getting quiet and waiting on God. I remind myself, God is sovereign . . . this is no accident. He has a plan and a purpose.

Although He was a Son,
He learned obedience from the things
which He suffered.

Hebrews 5:8

May 4

God works among the hosts of heaven. He works in the warp and woof, in the interwoven fabric, of everyday life. He works in people like you and me, in every generation, of every year.

We live our lives under the careful, loving, gracious, albeit sovereign, hand of our God. And the movements of time and history tick off according to His reckoning, exactly as He ordained.

My times
are in your hand.

Psalm 31:15

May 5

God keeps His promises. It's a major part of His immutable nature. He doesn't hold out hope with nice-sounding words, then renege on what He said He would do. God is neither fickle nor moody. And He never lies. As my own father used to say of people with integrity. "His word is His bond."

I will cry to God
Most High, to God who accomplishes
all things for me.

Psalm 57:2

May 6

When you deposit money in the bank, there's a limit on how much the FDIC will insure under one account ownership; usually it's about $100,000. But our infinite God has no limits. Millions upon multimillions of Christians can deposit themselves in His care, and He will make every one of them good. He will hold every one of us securely. No one can declare Him bankrupt of compassion or care. God will never say to anyone, "Sorry. We're full up. That's the limit. We can't guarantee more." You can entrust your soul to this "faithful Creator."

Let those also who suffer . . .
entrust their souls to a faithful Creator . . . .

1 Peter 4:19

May 7

What are you doing with the rest of your life? I'm talking about cultivating relationships, building memories that will help lift the load of future trials, and the deliberate pursuit of activities that will yield eternal dividends.

Do you have a family? Rather than leaving them the leftovers and crumbs and giving your job your best hours and your most creative ideas, how about rethinking the value of strengthening those ties? And while we're at it, let's not leave out necessary time for quietness, for personal reflection and refreshment.

There is precious treasure . . .
in the dwelling of the wise.

Proverbs 21:20

May 8

It isn't easy to trust God in times of adversity. Feelings of distress, despair, and darkness trouble our souls as we wonder if God truly cares about our plight. But *not to trust* Him is to doubt His sovereignty and to question His goodness. In order to trust God we must view our adverse circumstances through eyes of faith, not our senses.

It is only through Scripture, applied to our hearts by the Holy Spirit, that we receive the grace to trust God in everything.

We are not of those
who shrink back . . . but of those
who have faith.

Hebrews 10:39

May 9

God sees the events of life ahead of time—something which we of course can never do. We're great at history. Our hindsight is almost always 20/20. But we're lousy at prophecy, that is, the specifics of the future. Stop and think. We've no clue as to what will happen one minute from now, no idea what's going to happen next. But our invisible God, in His providence, is continually, constantly, and confidently at work.

He is the Lord of lords and
the King of kings, and those who are with Him
are the called and chosen and faithful.

Revelation 17:14

May 10

I've never seen skywriting that says, "I'm here, Chuck. You can count on Me." I've never heard an audible voice in the middle of the night reassuring me, "I'm here, My son." But by faith I see God and, inaudibly, I hear Him on a regular basis, reading Him written in the events of my life—whether it be the crushing blows that drive me to my knees or the joyous triumphs that send my heart winging. When I pause long enough to look back, I realize it is the unsearchable mind, . . . the irresistible providence of God at work, because He, though invisible, remains invincible.

Lo, I am with you always,
even to the end of the age.

Matthew 28:20

May 11

Some of you are going through trials right now that have dropped you on your knees. At the same time those trials are pulling you closer to the Lord than you've ever been in your life. That ought to bring rejoicing. You'll be more closely linked to Him. Some of the mysterious themes threaded through His Word will become clearer because you have been leveled by some unexpected affliction or enduring persecution or facing misunderstanding.

Thanks be to God . . . who . . .
manifests through us the sweet aroma of the
knowledge of Him in every place.

2 Corinthians 2:14

May 12

Be still . . . deliberately pause and discover that God is God. Stop reaching back into your own treasure of security. Stop trying to pull the strings yourself. Stop manipulating people and situations. Stop making excuses for your irresponsibilities. Stop ignoring reality. Stop rationalizing your way through life. *Stop all that!* How? You ask.

Initially: *Be quiet*. The immortal, invisible, all-wise God, hid from your eyes, is at work. Be very still and, for a change, listen.

In quietness and trust is your strength.

Isaiah 30:15

May 13

What about the day of Christ's return? On that glorious day, children will head off to school, loaded down with homework and peanut-butter-and-jelly sandwiches. Morning rush-hour traffic will choke the freeways. Merchants will be opening their doors to customers. Then, suddenly, in the twinkling of an eye, Christ will split the sky, and God's great plan for the future will suddenly take center stage. It could be tomorrow. *It could be today!* But whenever it is, that morning will begin as just another uneventful, ho-hum, no-big-deal kind of day.

The day of the Lord will come
like a thief. . . . Therefore be diligent.

2 Peter 3:10, 14

May 14

This is the wonder of God's sovereignty. Working behind the scenes, He is moving and pushing and rearranging events and changing minds until He brings out of even the most carnal and secular of settings a decision that will set His perfect plan in place.

Don't fall into the trap of thinking that God is asleep when it comes to nations, or that He is out of touch, or that He sits in heaven wringing His hands when it comes to godless rulers who make unfair, rash, or stupid decisions. Mark it down in permanent ink: God is always at work.

He makes the nations great,
then destroys them; He enlarges the nations,
then leads them away.

Job 12:23

May 15

The furnace of suffering provides not only light by which to examine our lives but heat to melt away the dross. Just as famine and financial ruin brought the prodigal son to his senses, so our trials bring us to our senses and draw us into the embrace of our Father. The common response to trials is resistance, if not outright resentment. How much better that we open the doors of our hearts and welcome the God-ordained trials as honored guests for the good they do in our lives.

You have been distressed by
various trials, so that the proof of your faith . . .
may be found to result in praise and glory.

1 Peter 1:6–7

May 16

There is nothing wrong with money earned honestly. Certainly there is nothing wrong in investing or giving or even spending money if the motive is right, if the heart is pure. But I have yet to discover anyone who has found true happiness simply in the gathering of more money. Although money is not sinful or suspect in itself, it is not what brings lasting contentment, fulfillment, or satisfaction.

How much better it is to get
wisdom than gold. And to get understanding
is to be chosen above silver.

Proverbs 16:16

MAY 17

In the Old Testament, God's hand symbolizes two things. The first is *discipline* (see Exod. 3:20, Job 30:21, and Ps. 32:4). The second is *deliverance* (see Deut. 9:26 and Ezek. 20:34). When we humble ourselves under the mighty hand of God, we willingly accept His discipline as being for our good and for His glory. Then we gratefully acknowledge His deliverance, which always comes in His time and in His way.

They are Your people . . .
whom You have brought out by Your . . .
outstretched arm.

DEUTERONOMY 9:29

May 18

You don't have to promote yourself if you've got the stuff. If you're good, if you are to be used of God, they'll find you. God will promote you. I don't care what the world system says. I urge you to let God do the promoting! Let God do the exalting! In the meantime, sit quietly under His hand. That's not popular counsel, I realize, but it sure works. Furthermore, you will never have to wonder in the future if it was you or the Lord who made things happen. And if He chooses to use you in a mighty way, really "exalt" you, you won't have any reason to get conceited. He did it all!

A humble spirit will obtain honor.

Proverbs 29:23

May 19

The secret to responsible trust is *acceptance.* Acceptance is taking from God's hand absolutely anything He gives, looking into His face in trust and thanksgiving, knowing that the confinement of the hedge we're in is good and for His glory. Even though what we're enduring may be painful, it's good simply because God Himself has allowed it. Acceptance is resting in God's goodness, believing that He has all things under His control—even people who are doing what is wrong. Yes . . . even wrongdoers.

Let us not lose heart in
doing good, for in due time we will reap
if we do not grow weary.

Galatians 6:9

May 20

Serenity is another word for peace; something we all long to have. But this peace isn't a nirvana hypnotic trance or something encountered by repeating a mantra a thousand times. It isn't acquired through yoga exercises or crystals or channeling or counsel from a guru in Tibet. Where do we find this peace? Peace comes from trusting in God.

The steadfast of mind
You will keep in perfect peace,
because he trusts in You.

Isaiah 26:3

May 21

We are all faced with a series of great opportunities, brilliantly disguised as unsolvable problems. Unsolvable without God's wisdom, that is. With His wisdom, they are changed to great opportunities. That change depends on our perspective. We are faced with a problem that seems to have no human solution. And perhaps it doesn't. There is no end in view. It has all the marks of an endlessly impossible situation. But I have found this is the platform upon which God does His greatest work. The more impossible the situation, the greater God accomplishes His work.

With God all things are possible.

Matthew 19:26

May 22

God is not known for doing standard things. He is engaged in doing very distinct things. When a person does something, it has the man or woman look about it. It drips with humanity. You can follow the logic of it and see the meaning behind it. You can even read what they paid for it and how they pulled it off and the organization that made it so slick. God doesn't build skyscrapers; men build skyscrapers. And they all have the touch of genius, human genius. But you cannot find a man who can make a star. And when God steps in, His working is like the difference between a skyscraper and a star.

He looks to the ends of the earth
and sees everything under the heavens.

Job 28:24

May 23

You know what? God personally cares about the things that worry us. He cares more about them than we care about them: those things that hang in our minds as nagging, aching, worrisome thoughts. First Peter 5:7 invites you to cast "all your anxiety on Him, because He has a care for you." He cares. You are His personal concern. He cares about those aching thoughts that are like heavy anchors dragging you down.

Casting all your anxiety
on Him, because He cares for you.

1 Peter 5:7

MAY 24

God is in no hurry.

We tend to think that if God is really engaged, He will change things within the next hour or so. Certainly by sundown. Absolutely by the end of the week. But God is not a slave to the human clock. Compared to the works of mankind, He is extremely deliberate and painfully slow. As religious poet George Herbert wisely penned, "God's mill grinds slow, but sure."

And now, LORD,
for what do I wait?
My hope is in You.

PSALM 39:7

May 25

As you walk the path of trust you will experience situations that simply defy explanation. When you look back, after the fact, you could never have figured out a better plan. At the time it seemed strange, mysterious . . . even illogical. Let me assure you, that's God working. Things will happen that seem to be totally contradictory, but these are God's arrangements. It was a wonderful day when I finally realized I don't have to explain or defend the will of God. My job is simply to obey it.

Do not tremble or be dismayed,
for the L*ORD* *your God is with you*
wherever you go.

Joshua 1:9

May 26

The hand of God holds you firmly in His control. The hand of God casts a shadow of the cross across your life. Sit down at the foot of that cross and deliberately submit your soul to His mighty hand. Accept His discipline. Acknowledge His deliverance. Ask for His discernment.

Then be quiet. Be still. Wait. And move over so I can sit beside you. I'm waiting too.

It does not depend on the
man who wills or the man who runs,
but on God who has mercy.

Romans 9:16

May 27

When the enemy knocks at the door or when he prowls around back or when he looks for the chink in your armor, you hang on to Christ. You stand firm in faith. You put on the "armor of God" (Eph. 6:11-20—please read it!). You have nothing to worry about. Nothing. For, as Peter reminds us, our Lord has "dominion forever and ever." He is the one ultimately in control, and that is something in which every believer can find strength to hope again.

To Him be
dominion forever and ever.

1 Peter 5:11

May 28

Work on a submissive spirit. Don't wait for the media to encourage you to do this . . . it'll never happen. Ask God, if necessary, to break the sinews of your will so that you become a person who is cooperative, submissive, harmonious, sympathetic, brotherly or sisterly, kindhearted in every area of this pilgrim life.

Remember, ultimately we are not submitting to human authority but to divine authority.

May the Lord cause you to
increase and abound in love for one another,
and for all people.

1 Thessalonians 3:12

May 29

No matter how dark the clouds, the sun will eventually pierce the darkness and dispel it; no matter how heavy the rain, the sun will ultimately prevail to hang a rainbow in the sky. Joy will chase away the clouds hovering over our faith and prevail over the disheartening trials that drench our lives.

Weeping may last
for the night, but a shout of joy
comes in the morning.

Psalm 30:5

May 30

We hear "heavenly" music today, and we think it's going to be like that in heaven. But actually, the most beautiful music on earth sounds like *Chopsticks* when placed alongside real heavenly music. Handel's *Hallelujah Chorus* will be nothing compared to the myriad of angels who will sing in antiphonal voice as we join them in praises to the Lamb of God.

I heard the voice of many angels . . .
saying with a loud voice, "Worthy is the Lamb
that was slain to receive power and riches . . .
and glory and blessing."

Revelation 5:11–12

May 31

God's plans are not hindered when the events of this world are carnal or secular. His presence penetrates, regardless. He is not limited to working in the Christian family. He is as much at work in the Oval Office as He is in your pastor's study. He is as much at work in other countries of the world, like Iran or China or the Middle East, as He is in America. To doubt that is to draw boundaries around His sovereign control.

All the kings of the earth will
give thanks to You, O Lord, when they have
heard the words of Your mouth.

Psalm 138:4

June

We know
who holds the future.

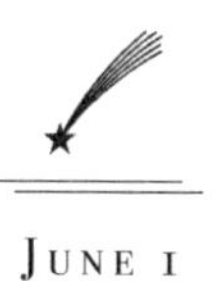

June 1

I'm a firm believer in saving, investing, intelligent spending, and wise money management. But I have trouble finding one word of scriptural support for being a tightwad! Never have I seen one who could dream broad dreams or see vast visions of what God can do in spite of man's limitations.

Give me a handful of "greathearts" . . . generous, openhanded, visionary, spiritually minded givers . . . magnanimous giants with God who get excited about abandoning themselves to Him.

A generous man devises
generous things, and by generosity he shall stand.

Isaiah 32:8, NKJV

June 2

It is a waste of time trying to unscrew the inscrutable workings of God. You'll never be able to do it. That's simply the way God works. He honors faith and obedience. He will honor your faith if you will trust Him in a walk of obedience. And when you trust Him completely, you will enjoy inner quietness and security. You will have a secure confidence that you are walking in His will. You will be surrounded by His peace.

We must obey
God rather than men.

Acts 5:29

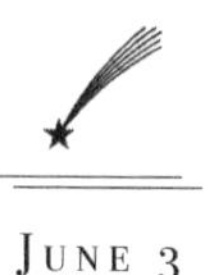

June 3

When you worry about what you don't have, you won't be able to enjoy what you do have. That's what Jesus was talking about in Matthew 6:25: "I say to you, do not be anxious for your life, as to what you shall eat, or what you shall drink. . . ." Worry is assuming responsibilities that you cannot handle. The truth is, they are responsibilities that God never intended for you to handle, because they are His.

I say to you, do not be anxious
for your life, as to what you shall eat,
or what you shall drink. . . .

Matthew 6:25

June 4

What are the benefits of realizing God Incomprehensible? We no longer reduce Him to manageable terms. We are no longer tempted to manipulate Him and His will . . . or defend Him and His ways. We get new glimpses of Him "lofty and exalted," surrounded by legions of seraphim who witness Him as the "Lord of hosts" as they shout forth His praises in antiphonal voice.

Holy, Holy, Holy,
is the Lord of hosts.

Isaiah 6:3

June 5

God trains His best personnel—in obscurity. Men and women of God, servant-leaders in the making, are first unknown, unseen, unappreciated, and unapplauded. In the relentless demands of obscurity, character is built. Strange as it may seem, those who first accept the silence of obscurity are best qualified to handle the applause of popularity.

The God of peace . . .
equip you in every good thing
to do His will.

Hebrews 13:20–21

June 6

Behind the scenes, before He ever flung the stars into space, God had today in mind. He had this very week in mind. In fact, He had you in mind. And He knew exactly what He was going to do. God is never at a loss to know what He's going to do in our situations. He knows perfectly well what is best for us.

I will once again
deal marvelously with this people,
wondrously marvelous.

Isaiah 29:14

June 7

God has some extremely exciting things in mind for His children. For some it may happen tomorrow. For some it may happen next month or next year or five years down the road. We don't know when. For some . . . it could happen today. But the beautiful thing about this adventure called faith is that we can count on Him never to lead us astray. He knows exactly where He's taking us. Our job is to obey.

I will strengthen you,
surely I will help you, surely I will uphold
you with My righteous right hand.

Isaiah 41:10

June 8

God's hand is not so short that it cannot save, nor is His ear so heavy that He cannot hear. Whether you see Him or not, He is at work in your life this very moment. God specializes in turning the mundane into the meaningful. God not only moves in unusual ways, He also moves on uneventful days. He is just as involved in the mundane events as He is in the miraculous. One of my longtime friends, Howie Stevenson, often says with a smile, "God moves among the casseroles."

He will exult over you with joy,
He will be quiet in His love.

Zephaniah 3:17

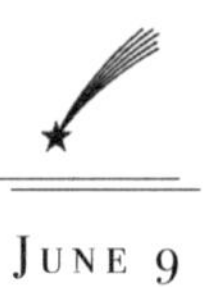

June 9

Verbal restraint is fast becoming a forgotten virtue. Thanks to tell-all tabloids and hide-nothing television talk shows, nothing is restrained. When was the last time anyone in the media blushed? Yet restraint and control always work in your favor. Learn to keep confidences, especially the confidences of your family, and your friends. Come to be known for keeping secrets! It's part of having character marked by strength and dignity.

Wise men store up knowledge,
but with the mouth of the foolish,
ruin is at hand.

PROVERBS 10:14

June 10

Someone has said, "Education is going from an unconscious to conscious awareness of one's ignorance." I agree. No one has a corner on wisdom. All the name-dropping in the world does not heighten the significance of our character. If anything, it reduces it. Our acute need is to cultivate a willingness to learn and to remain teachable. Learning from our children. Learning from friends. Learning even from our enemies. How beautiful it is to find a servant-hearted, teachable spirit among those who occupy high-profile positions of authority.

The fruit of the righteous is
a tree of life, and he who is wise wins souls.

Proverbs 11:30

June 11

Ask God. Trust God. We are completely dependent on Him for eternal life, for forgiveness, for character, for security. His light in our life gives us a growing disgust for things that merely satisfy the flesh. It shows us the importance of character, the incredible change that can come by standing alone on the things of God. He alone can give us grace and winsomeness and keep us from becoming squint-eyed, cranky Christians.

This hope we have as an
anchor of the soul, a hope both
sure and steadfast.

Hebrews 6:19

June 12

The grace of a woman brings her a place of honor. An excellent wife accords her husband a place of significance, publicly and personally. A prudent wife is a gift from God, better than any earthly inheritance. Such a woman gives her husband prudent counsel and provides her family with the leadership of reason and good sense.

There is strength of character and an aura of dignity about the godly woman that cannot be found even among godly men.

Strength and dignity are her clothing,
and she smiles at the future.

Proverbs 31:25

June 13

Life and pain are synonymous. You cannot have one without the other. Pain is a fact of life in this fallen world, and we cannot escape it. In fact, the goal in life is not to get away from the pain of it, but to endure through it, in fact, to triumph over it, while learning the lessons only pain can teach us.

As someone put it, "Pain is inevitable. Misery is optional." Since we cannot get free of pain, the secret of successful living is finding ways to live above the level of misery. Indeed, we must.

My flesh and my heart may fail,
but God is the strength of my heart.

Psalm 73:26

June 14

God's grace sees beyond our deepest need. He meets us where we are, talking straight to us in terms that even we can understand. He does this through His Word.

We need God's great grace to clear our hearts of all malice. He can give us the ability to turn our pain over to Him in this life, enabling us to resist all attempts at getting even, while He, through His power, deals with this unsolvable problem for us.

If anyone is in Christ,
he is a new creature, the old things passed away;
behold, new things have come.

2 Corinthians 5:17

June 15

God is looking at your town, your city, your neighborhood, and He's looking for His people to whom He can say, "You are Mine. I want to use you there. Because you proved yourself faithful there." The only difference is our geography. Our calling is to be faithful in the demanding tasks, whether that is our education, our marriage, our occupation, or just the daily grind of life. That's the kind of men and women God wants to use.

Who is among you that
fears the LORD, ., . . let him trust in the name
of the LORD and rely on his God.

Isaiah 50:10

June 16

God magnifies HIS name when we are weak. We don't have to be eloquent or strong or handsome. We don't have to be beautiful or brilliant or have all the answers to be blessed of God. He honors our faith. All He asks is that we trust Him, that we stand before Him in integrity and faith, and He'll win the battle.

He who walks in
integrity walks securely.

Proverbs 10:9

June 17

It is God's love for us that causes Him to bring us to an end of our own strength. He sees our need to trust Him, and His love is so great that He will not let us live another day without turning over our arms to Him, our fears, our worries, even our confusion, so that nothing becomes more significant to us than our Father.

Never, ever forget it: The battle is the Lord's!

The battle is the LORD'S and
He will give you into our hands.

1 Samuel 17:47

June 18

Living for Christ is the most exciting adventure in the world. But it's hard. It's a lot easier to punch your enemy's lights out . . . to devise ways to fight back, to get even, because that satisfies your flesh. It's a lot easier to keep than to give, because that comes naturally. It's a lot easier to work up your own suspicion, and when he's not looking, whomp, get in your stroke. But that's not God's way . . . and that's not best.

Be peaceable, gentle, showing
every consideration for all men.

Titus 3:2

June 19

Worry is a complete waste of energy. It solves nothing. That's why Jesus said, "Which of you by worrying can add one cubit to his stature?" In essence He was saying, "You go to bed tonight and fret and fuss because you're not five feet, eleven inches; you're only five feet, nine inches. But when you wake up in the morning, you're still going to be five feet, nine inches." Worry will never make you stretch! And it won't solve that anxiety on your mind either.

Which of you by worrying
can add one cubit to his stature?

Matthew 6:27

June 20

In an overpopulated world, it's easy to underestimate the significance of one. There are so many people who have so many gifts and skills who are already doing so many things that are so important, who needs me? What can I as one individual contribute to the overwhelming needs of our world?

But the truth is, you are you—the only you in all the world.

You are He who brought me
forth from the womb; You made me trust
when upon my mother's breasts.

Psalm 22:9

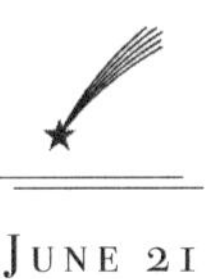

June 21

When I read God's Word, I don't find that many stories about great crusades and city-wide revivals and mass meetings where God's attention rested on an entire country or a whole community. More often, I find individual men and women who made a difference, who set the pace or cut a wide swath or stood in the gap and changed their times. From Genesis to Revelation, we see God's hand on the lives of individuals who thought and said and did what was right—regardless—and as a result, history was made.

He who plants and he who waters
are one. . . . We are God's fellow workers.

1 Corinthians 3:8–9

June 22

Every achievement worth remembering is stained with the blood of diligence and scarred by the wounds of disappointment. To quit, to run, to escape, to hide—none of these options solve anything. They only postpone the acceptance of, and reckoning with, reality. . . .

Battles are won in the trenches . . . in the grit and grime of courageous determination . . . in the arena of life, day in and day out, amidst the smell of sweat and the cry of anguish.

Be steadfast, immovable,
always abounding in the work of the Lord,
knowing that your toil is not in vain.

1 Corinthians 15:58

June 23

Suffering pushes us out of our homes. It puts us in touch with our neighbors. As my brother, Orville, stated after losing so much when Hurricane Andrew swept across southern Florida, "It blew down all our fences and we finally got to meet all our neighbors!" Hardship forces us to grab hands with one another and pull up closer together. Suffering never ruined a nation! Hardship doesn't fracture families. Affluence does!

Even if I am being poured out
as a drink offering upon the sacrifice and
service of your faith, I rejoice and share
my joy with you all.

Philippians 2:17

JUNE 24

Does it matter if you get involved or not? It matters greatly—it matters to your character!

Numerous needs and issues surround us. They summon us to stand up and be counted. While we will not be able to respond to all of them, the solution is not to respond to any of them! So let me ask you: When are you going to stand up, to stand alone, to answer the call of God in this hour?

Set your mind on
the things above, not on the things
that are on earth.

COLOSSIANS 3:2

June 25

When the temptation to worry first arrives, that's the critical moment. The tendency is to entertain it. To let it onto the front porch and allow it to sit there. But before you know it, worry has crawled in through the window and made itself at home! No, worry must be stopped. We have to decide that we are going to commit this worry to God right now and refuse to entertain it, even on the front porch of our thinking.

This is the confidence
which we have before Him, that,
if we ask anything according to His will,
He hears us.

1 John 5:14

June 26

Walking with God is the most exciting and rewarding of all experiences on earth. I should add, it is also the most difficult. I don't think I've ever met an exception to the rule, that those who walk closest to God are those who, like Jesus, become acquainted with trials and testings. God takes us through struggles and difficulties so that we might become increasingly more committed to Him.

Do not be surprised at the
fiery ordeal among you, which comes
upon you for your testing.

1 Peter 4:12

June 27

We don't hear much about hanging in there and persevering . . . about staying power! But there is more to it than merely enduring. It's one thing to stand grim-faced, tightfisted, and staring at God with anger, saying, "How DARE YOU! What right do You have?" or "Look at what I've done for you! And look at what I get in return!" That's one kind of perseverance. But there's another kind. The kind that stands with an open hand and open arms, that looks into the face of God and replies, "I submit myself to You."

Blessed is a man who
perseveres under trial; for . . . he will
receive the crown of life.

James 1:12

June 28

When the sovereign God brings us to nothing, it is to reroute our lives, not to end them. Human perspective says, "Aha, you've lost this, you've lost that. You've caused this, you've caused that. You've ruined this, you've ruined that." But God says, "No. No. It's time to reroute your life. Now's the time to start anew!"

The steps of a man
are established by the Lord,
and He delights in his way.

Psalm 37:23

June 29

Whatever you do when conflicts arise, be wise. If you're not careful, you will handle conflicts in the energy of the flesh. And then . . . you'll be sorry.

What do I mean by being wise? Well, look at the whole picture. Fight against jumping to quick conclusions and seeing only your side. Look both ways. Weigh the differences. There are always two sides on the streets of conflict. Look both ways. Weigh the differences.

The mind of the prudent
acquires knowledge, and the ear
of the wise seeks knowledge.

Proverbs 18:15

June 30

The only hope we have is daily dependence on the living Lord. It's the only way we can make it. He's touched with our feelings of infirmity, our weaknesses, our inability in the dark and lonely times to say no. He's touched with that. And He says, "I'm ready with all the power you need. Call on Me and I'll give you what you need."

So? Call on Him! Stop this moment and call on Him. He will hear and heed your cry.

Say to those with anxious heart,
"Take courage, fear not. Behold, your God . . .
will save you."

Isaiah 35:4

JULY

Surprises are part of God's plan. They remind us He's still in charge.

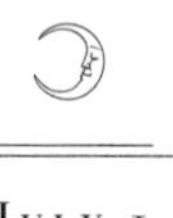

July 1

Does one person make a difference? Let me ask you, did Christ? God so loved the world that He did something. He didn't select a committee. He didn't theorize how great it would be for someone to come to our rescue. He didn't simply grieve over our waywardness and wring His hands in sorrow. He did something! And, in turn, the Son of God said to God the Father, "I will go." He did something about it.

For God so loved the world,
that He gave His only begotten son,
that whoever believes in Him shall not perish,
but have eternal life.

John 3:16

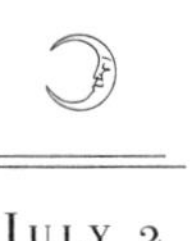

July 2

Time spreads itself before us, directionless and vacant. That time can be filled with meaningful activities and personal accomplishments, but in order for that to occur, you must think through a plan and carry it out. You do not have to plan or follow through. Time neither requires it nor demands it. If, however, you hope to look back over those days, weeks, months, and years and smile at what was achieved, planning is required.

There is an appointed time
for everything. And there is a time for
every event under heaven.

Ecclesiastes 3:1

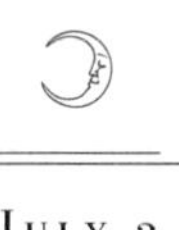

July 3

God counsels us with His eye. The eye makes no sound when it moves. It requires a sensitive earthly eye to watch the movement of the eye of God—God's directions. All He may do is turn your attention in another direction. But that's all you may need. When you wait, you listen. You pore over a favorite passage in His Word. You quietly give attention to His presence and to His direction.

I will instruct you and teach you
in the way which you should go; I will
counsel you with My eye upon you.

Psalm 32:8

July 4

We get in a hurry when we don't wait on the Lord. We jump ahead and do rash things. We shoot from the hip. We run off at the mouth, saying things that we later regret. But when we have sufficiently waited on the Lord, He gets full control of our spirit. At such moments, we're like a glove, and His hand is moving us wherever He pleases. Having known that experience, I can testify, there's nothing to compare it to. It's marvelous!

Let your heart keep my commandments;
for length of days and years of life and peace
they will add to you.

Proverbs 3:1-2

July 5

Fears lurk in the shadows of every area of life. Perhaps you've suddenly discovered that an unexpected addition to your family is on the way. Don't be afraid. God can enable you to handle four kids just like He helped you handled three. You may be uncertain where your job is leading. The future may look very threatening. You are uneasy about what's around the corner. Or perhaps you have a doctor's appointment pending and you are afraid of what the exam might reveal. Jesus says, "Stop being afraid. Trust Me!"

Commit yourself
to the Lord; let Him deliver. . . .

Psalm 22:8

July 6

I want to encourage those of you who have become rather concerned about the fine print of your life. I want to commend you for that. You are the ones who make godly husbands and godly roommates and godly wives and godly workmen and godly pastors and godly musicians and godly professionals. You care enough about your life that regardless of your occupation, when you hear something declared from Scripture, you're thinking, *How can I get that into my life?* Good for you!

I shall delight in
Your commandments, which I love.

Psalm 119:47

July 7

It is during the interludes of life that we have time to seize a dream or an ideal objective. Some of you in a quiet moment of your life realized the vocation into which God was calling you. Maybe it happened at a camp or a retreat, where you threw a branch of promise on the fire. Maybe it happened in the quietness of your own room after a church service one evening.

You have to slow down and become quiet in those special times to hear His voice, to sense His leading.

Seek the LORD and His strength;
seek His face continually.

Psalm 105:4

July 8

It's important that every once in a while we sit down, take a long look at our short lives, and just count our blessings. Who are we to have been protected from the rains that fell, leaving hundreds homeless? Who are we that He has blessed our house and kept it safe? Warm in the winter . . . cool in the summer. Who am I, Lord, that You should give me health and strength to be able to hold a job or pursue this career or get this degree? Who am I?

Who am I, O Lord God, . . .
that You have brought me this far?

2 Samuel 7:18

July 9

Our most difficult times are not when things are going hard. Hard times create dependent people. You don't get proud when you're dependent on God. Survival keeps you humble. Pride happens when everything is swinging in your direction. When you've just received that promotion, when you look back and you can see an almost spotless record in the last number of months or years, when you're growing in prestige and fame and significance, that's the time to watch out . . . especially if you're unaccountable.

The Lord is good
to those who wait for Him, to the
person who seeks Him.

Lamentations 3:25

July 10

When you wait on the Lord, you don't have to sit in a corner contemplating your navel, or walk around in a daze humming "Sweet Hour of Prayer."

Sometimes, of course, you need to sit down quietly, by yourself, alone with the Lord for a time of quietness. Solitude and silence are wonderful when nourishing our souls. But mostly you go right on with your business. You press on with your regular activities. You just focus more fully on the Lord in the midst of it. You stay preoccupied with Him.

Trust in Him always,
O people; pour your heart out before Him;
God is a refuge for us.

Psalm 62:8

July 11

When preparing for an unprecedented event, wait on the Lord before getting involved. At least as important as the thing we are waiting for is the work God does in us while we wait. He works on our patience. He works on our circumstances. He works on others. If we plunge in, if we run ahead, we foul up His better arrangements and plans.

If you're on the verge of a big decision, wait. In fact, I've found the bigger the decision, the longer the wait. Don't get in a hurry.

If any of you lacks wisdom,
let him ask of God who gives to all generously and
without reproach, and it will be given to him.

James 1:5

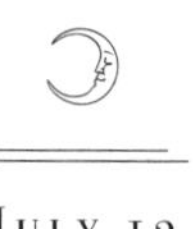

July 12

When no one else notices, mark it down, God notices. When no one else remembers, God records. The psalmist tells us that He even keeps our tears in a bottle. He will reward us for acts that are done in His name. So be encouraged. There will come a day when rewards will come your way as they should, perhaps not on this earth, . . . but someday.

You have taken account
of my wanderings; put my tears
in Your bottle.

Psalm 56:8

July 13

We must admit that we spend more of our time concentrating and fretting over the things that can't be changed—than we do giving attention to the one that we can change, our choice of attitude. Stop and think about some of the things that suck up our attention and energy, all of them inescapable: the weather, the wind, people's action and criticisms, who won or lost the game, delays at airports.

Quit wasting energy fighting the inescapable and turn your energy to keeping the right attitude.

O Lord, my heart is not proud,
nor my eyes haughty; nor do I involve
myself in great matters.

Psalm 131:1

July 14

Jesus Christ stands at the door. He holds out His hands that are scarred. His feet are pierced, and He bears in His body the marks of death. He says, "I know the pressure you are under. I understand the strain. I know the unfair abuse. But let me offer you some encouragement. Don't be afraid. Look at life through My eyes! Stop letting life intimidate you! Stop running scared. Trust Me!"

My heart is steadfast,
O God, my heart is steadfast.

Psalm 57:7

July 15

Does God care about the number of hairs in your scalp? Does He care if a sparrow falls? Yes, His Word assures us He does. Then be assured of this: He's a specialist in the things that worry you down inside. The things you dread tomorrow or this coming week. The things that make you wonder, "How can I get this together?" God's reassurance to you is, "Look, that's what I specialize in. . . . Bring all of it to me. Ask Me to take charge."

You do not have
because you do not ask.

James 4:2

July 16

When we talk about perfect trust, we're talking about what gives us roots, character, the stability to handle the hard times. Trusting God doesn't alter our circumstances. Perfect trust in Him changes us. It doesn't make life all rosy and beautiful and neat and lovely and financially secure and comfortable. But trust that is rooted in an abiding faith in God makes all that real in us—secure, relaxed, and calm against insuperable odds.

My soul takes refuge in You;
and in the shadow of Your wings
I will take refuge.

Psalm 57:1

July 17

Grace means that God, in forgiving you, gives you the strength to endure the consequences. Grace frees us so that we can obey our Lord. It does not mean sin's consequences are automatically removed. If I sin and in the process of sinning break my arm, when I find forgiveness from sin, I still have to deal with a broken bone.

But thanks be to God
that though you were slaves of sin,
you became obedient from the heart.

Romans 6:17

July 18

We have set ourselves up with a sin mind-set. We have told ourselves that grace means those consequences are all instantly removed, so we let ourselves be sucked under by the power of the flesh, rather than believing what Paul teaches, that we don't have to sin day after day after day. We sin because we want to. We have the power in the person of the Holy Spirit to say no to it at every turn in our life. If we choose to say yes against the prompting of the Holy Spirit, we may be certain we will live in the backwash of the consequences.

That I . . . may be found in Him,
not having a righteousness of my own . . .
but that which is through faith in Christ.

Philippians 3:8–9

July 19

When we go through periods of deep distress . . . it is wise—in fact, it is biblical—not to surround ourselves with people, no matter how well-meaning they might be. Solitude is essential. Silence is necessary. Words from others usually distract. Stay in the Lord's presence and seek His mind during this painful time.

In the soul-searching of our lives, we are to stay quiet so we can hear Him say all that He wants to say to us in our hearts.

Let all who take
refuge in You be glad.

Psalm 5:11

July 20

Those servants who refuse to get bogged down in and anchored to the past are those who pursue the objectives of the future. People who do this are seldom petty. They are too involved in getting a job done to be occupied with yesterday's hurts and concerns. Very near the end of his . . . life, Paul wrote: "I have fought the good fight, I have finished the course, I have kept the faith." What a grand epitaph! He seized every day by the throat. He relentlessly pursued life.

I have fought the good fight,
I have finished the course,
I have kept the faith.

2 Timothy 4:7

July 21

It is easy to anticipate that this year will be very much like last and the one before it, when, in fact, chances are good it will be altogether different. So when events begin to turn, realize that none of it is merely coincidental. Remember that. Take the word "coincidental" out of your vocabulary, along with "luck." You can trash them both! You don't need them anymore. Nothing is coincidental! "Luck" has no place in a Christian's vocabulary.

Praise the name
of the LORD *your God, who has dealt*
wondrously with you.

Joel 2:26

July 22

Don't ever try to convince me that some situation in this life is absolutely permanent. God can move an entire nation. He can change the mind of your stubborn mate. He can move in the affairs of your community. No barrier is too high, no chasm is too wide for Him, because He is not limited by space or time, by the visible or the invisible. Remember, He lives in a realm that transcends all that. He is all-powerful. And when God is ready to move, He moves.

I know that my Redeemer lives,
and at the last He will take His
stand on the earth.

Job 19:25

July 23

God gave you a mind. God gave you reason. God gave you a unique sensitivity; it's built into your spiritual system, and each person's system is tuned differently. God wants to reveal His will to you and to teach you while you are waiting. . . . Get into His Word. Get on your knees. Accept counsel from those who are maturing and balanced believers, solidly biblical in their theology and in their own life. And wait.

We walk by faith,
not by sight.

2 Corinthians 5:7

July 24

More often than not, when something looks like it's the absolute end, it is really the beginning.

Think of the cross. The Roman officials applauded. The Jewish officials rejoiced. "Finally, we got rid of him, that troublemaker! We're glad that's over." Yet three days later, He was alive again. What seemed like an ending was only the beginning.

He who sits on the throne said,
"Behold, I am making all things new."

Revelation 21:5

July 25

The best synonym for self-control is "discipline." Interesting word *self-control.* We use it often but rarely analyze it, even when we come across it in the Bible. Self-control means "inner strength."

The fruit of the Spirit is self-control. Self-control frees us from slavery. Self-control stops bad habits. It checks us. It halts us. When it comes to retaliation, self-control restrains us. Without it, we gear up to get even.

If we live by the Spirit,
let us also walk by the Spirit.

Galatians 5:25

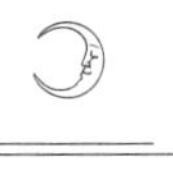

July 26

You know one of the most encouraging things about faith? *It pleases God. . . .* That's why I want to encourage you: Walk by faith! Stop this plagued biting of nails and weariness of worry that you encourage within when the tests come. Relax! Learn to say, "Lord, this is Your battle. This is Your need that You've allowed me to trust You for. And I'm waiting for You to do it. I'm willing to wait as long as necessary for You to do the impossible."

Without faith it is
impossible to please Him.

Hebrews 11:6

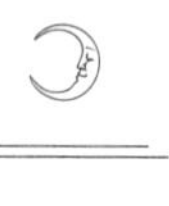

July 27

God, alone is worthy of our worship and praise. Being sovereign, He is in charge of all life! The day we resign ourselves to that is the day we really begin to understand what it means to rest by faith in a living God through Jesus Christ. When I don't fathom why, He knows. When I haven't a clue as to when, He understands. And when I cannot imagine good coming from something, He brings it to pass.

Your righteousness, O God,
reaches to the heavens, You who
have done great things.

Psalm 71:19

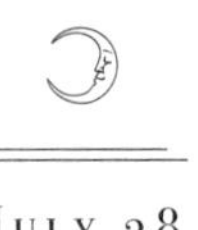

July 28

As Christians we live a life that is different—morally excellent, ethically beautiful. It's called a holy life. And God honors that. Because it's like He is.

All of our Christian lives we have sung the old hymn "Take Time to Be Holy." Those words are true. It does take time to be holy. It certainly takes time to be mature. It takes time to cultivate a walk with the Lord. God has called us to be holy, so let's be holy.

Be imitators of God,
as beloved children.

Ephesians 5:1

July 29

It may be the most difficult time in your life. You may be enduring your own whirlwind . . . or you may be the innocent bystander caught in the consequential backwash of another's sin. You may feel desperately alone, and it may seem that it will never, ever end. But believe me, the whirlwind is a temporary experience. Your faithful, caring Lord will see you through it.

Great is Your faithfulness.

Lamentations 3:23

July 30

The poet Samuel Taylor Coleridge once described friendship as "a sheltering tree." What a beautiful description of that special relationship. As I read those words, I think of my friends as great leafy trees, who spread themselves over me, providing shade from the sun, whose presence is a stand against the blast of winter's wind of loneliness. A great, sheltering tree; that's a friend.

There is a friend who
sticks closer than a brother.

Proverbs 18:24

July 31

Imagine someone who is giving you grief. It may be one of your grown, wayward children. Maybe it's someone who represents a formidable presence. . . . Stubborn person, right? Strong-hearted individual, correct? Imagine that heart that is so hard, so granite-like, changing into soft putty in the hands of the Lord. It's possible! There is no heart so stubborn that it cannot become breakable in the hands of the Lord.

Every man's way is
right in his own eyes, but the LORD
weighs the hearts.

PROVERBS 21:2

AUGUST

When we
know Who, we can stop
asking "Why?"

August 1

The world doesn't forgive. It doesn't say, "I understand. I've done what you've done a dozen times myself. I know you're sorry, and I certainly forgive you. It's OK." Instead, the world gets back in like measure—and preferably in greater measure.

But Christians are not to do that. We are to be different. We are not to set our standards according to this world. We are not to be conformed.

Do not be conformed
to this world, but be transformed by
the renewing of your mind.

Romans 12:2

AUGUST 2

God will be all in all. God will have His way. What seems frustrating and wrong and unfair is not the end of the story. It's just the end of a chapter. The book He is writing has many, many chapters. Augustine was correct, absolutely right when he said, "We count on God's mercy for our past mistakes; we count on God's love for our present needs; but we count on God's sovereignty for the future."

Draw near to God and
He will draw near to you.

JAMES 4:8

AUGUST 3

Friends are not neutral; they impact our lives. If your friends lead good lives, they encourage you to become a better person. If your friends lead disreputable lives, they lead you down the same path—or worse. . . . So choose your friends carefully and wisely. Gossips usually gravitate to gossips. Rebels run with rebels. You want to be wise? Choose wise friends.

Be not deceived:
Bad company corrupts
good morals.

1 CORINTHIANS 15:33

August 4

Our typical human response to offense is to try all the wrong things: silence, resentment, grudge, indifference, even plotting a way to maneuver and manipulate to get our offender in a vulnerable spot so we can twist the verbal knife, once we've plunged it in. None of this pleases God . . . nor does it work!

We need a heart of full forgiveness and grace in our family relationships, in our work and school relationships, certainly in our church relationships.

To one who knows the right
thing to do and does not do it,
to him it is sin.

James 4:17

August 5

All of us have our own particular fears. Fear of darkness. Fear of failure. Fear of the unknown. Fear of heights. Fear of financial disaster. Fear of sickness. Fear of death. You name it, we entertain it. Yet, God promises to deliver us from all our fears . . . and so it stands to reason that we can rest in Him. He shields us when we take refuge in Him.

The word of the Lord
is tested; He is a shield to those
who take refuge in Him.

2 Samuel 22:31

August 6

God hears our cry. He lifts us up out of a horrible pit; He places our feet upon a rock and establishes our going. He proves Himself strong in our weakness; He sheds light in our darkness; He becomes hope in our uncertainty and security in our confusion. He is the Centerpiece of our lives.

The LORD is my
light and my salvation;
whom shall I fear?

Psalm 27:1

August 7

Every individual has a purpose for living—every one of us. No one God brings to life on this earth is insignificant. The tragedy of all tragedies is that we should live and die having never found that purpose, that special, God-ordained reason for serving our generation, You have, like no other person on this planet, particular contributions that you are to make to this generation. They may not be as great as your dreams, or they might be far beyond your expectations; but whatever they are, you are to find them and carry them out.

Let us examine and probe
our ways. . . . We lift up our heart and hands
toward God in heaven.

Lamentations 3:40–41

August 8

My soul is not on the run. My spirit has not capsized, because in the Lord I take refuge. A refuge is a place of hiding. It is a place of protection. The term for refuge is *chasah* in the ancient Hebrew. A chasah is a protective place that provides safety from that which would otherwise hit and hurt. It's a protection from danger and from distress.

In the Lord
I take refuge.

Psalm 11:1

August 9

It's the only solution I have found to retaliation and revenge—the only way I've been able to get past blame and resentment, the only antidote for secret, smoldering feelings of rage from the pain of my past. . . . Forgiveness.

Not until I fully forgave my offenders, one by one, name by name, offense by offense, do I "gain the mastery" over those tendencies within me to get back or get even.

Be harmonious, sympathetic,
brotherly, kindhearted and humble in spirit.

1 Peter 3:8

August 10

The enemy of our souls loves to taunt us with past failures, wrongs, disappointments, disasters, and calamities. And if we let him continue doing this, our life becomes a long and dark tunnel, with very little light at the end.

Fortunately, God has given us a magnificent solution that can make a difference. I call these fourteen words the secret of celebrating life:

Forgetting what lies behind and
reaching forward to what lies ahead,
I press on. . . .

Philippians 3:13–14

August 11

One of the great themes of Christianity is triumphant hope. Not just hope as in a distant, vague dream, but triumphant hope, the kind of hope where all things end right. In the midst of the struggles and the storms and the sufferings of life, we can advance our thoughts beyond today and see relief . . . triumph . . . victory. Because, in the end, God does indeed win.

I am the LORD your God,
who upholds your right hand, who says to you,
"Do not fear, I will help you."

ISAIAH 41:13

August 12

There is no quality more godlike than humility. Remember that when the next promotion comes. Remember that when God selects you as one of His unique spokespersons and places you in a position where the public looks up to you and listens to you. Remember the importance of humility of heart and mind. Nothing is more admirable, more godlike than being willing to live our true humility . . . without calling attention to it.

An arrogant man stirs up strife,
but he who trusts in the LORD will prosper.

Proverbs 28:25

August 13

God is our refuge, and what comfort that brings! He is your refuge when you awaken in the night filled with fear, and cold sweat breaks out. He is your refuge, your strength, a very present help when events transpire that you cannot understand. . . . When you read the next headline, and it tells of some event that you and I would call tragic, He is a very present help.

God is our
refuge and strength, a very
present help in trouble.

Psalm 46:1

August 14

Our God is in sovereign control of all the events of this earth. . . .

Then how can I explain why bad things happen? How can I resolve the ringing question, "Why, God?"

I did not say our Father has explained Himself. . . . I said our Father has planned or permitted the events of this earth. He has no obligation to explain Himself. The Creator does not explain why to the created. It would be like a brilliant potter explaining himself to a mass of soft clay.

Job answered the LORD and said,
"I know that You can do all things,
and that no purpose of Yours
can be thwarted."

JOB 42:1

AUGUST 15

The place of highest exaltation, as we see in the Lord Jesus Christ, is a place of self-emptying humility. It's not a phony-baloney style of fake piety. It's true humility of mind. It's putting the other person first. It's sharing and sharing alike. It is giving up as well as building up. It is enjoying the pleasures of another's promotion. It is applauding God's hand in other lives. It is quickly forgetting one's own clippings. It is being like Christ.

Being found in appearance
as a man, He humbled Himself
by becoming obedient. . . .

PHILIPPIANS 2:8

August 16

We live in a world where we take care of our own. We look out for number one. But God's plan encompasses everyone. Every nation. Every race. All cultures. Huge, highly developed countries, but not excluding the small, struggling ones. His message of shalom through faith in Christ is universal. Unlimited. Without prejudice. Vast!

There is salvation in no one else;
for there is no other name under heaven
that has been given among men by
which we must be saved.

Acts 4:12

August 17

Hope is a wonderful gift from God, a source of strength and courage in the face of life's harshest trials.

When we are trapped in a tunnel of misery, hope points to the light at the end.

When we are overworked and exhausted, hope gives us fresh energy.

When we are discouraged, hope lifts our spirits.

When we are tempted to quit, hope keeps us going.

Whom have I in heaven but You?
And besides You, I desire nothing on earth.

Psalm 73:25

August 18

Nothing surprises God. What puzzles us is permitted by our Lord, for reasons too profound to grasp. It is put together in the counsel of His own will so that it fits perfectly into His plan for His glory and for His purposes. As His servant, I say in response, "I will not fear. Though I don't understand it, I will not fear. Though You take something that's deeply significant to me, though You allow a catastrophe to strike, I will not fear. I will not blame, I will not doubt, and I will not question."

Cease striving,
and know that I am God.

Psalm 46:10

August 19

We shall encounter enemy attacks in any number of areas. While we ought not to live in fear of it, we're not to be ignorant of it either. The enemy loves for you to be kept ignorant about him, to think of him inaccurately or with a shrug. . . .

Do you need some good news? We can resist the enemy! His attacks may be directed toward the vulnerable part of your life, but the shield of faith will protect you from them. You can resist him!

But resist [the enemy],
firm in your faith. . . .

1 Peter 5:9

August 20

God, our loving, caring, faithful, holy, and just God, has shaped a plan that will lead to victory, hope, peace, and joy. All of it takes shape under His mighty hand, as we surrender our wills to His. It happens under His hand. Get that. And under His hand we give up what we want. We surrender our wishes and desires, as we accept His plan. In the process, He is glorified. And because of His grace, many rewards come our way. The blessings just keep coming like waves on the seashore. And they come at "the proper time," because His timing is always right.

Humble yourselves . . .
under God's mighty hand, that he
may lift you up in due time.

1 Peter 5:6, niv

August 21

Don't let it bother you that you are different. That's what makes you unique. It gives extra value to your intelligence. That's what puts you in demand. Don't care how others run their companies; run yours right. Don't care if most of the people walk away from danger; you walk toward it. You do what's right. Don't lie. Don't cheat. Don't steal. Don't hang around with people who do. It takes courage to swim upstream, against the current. Do it!

The fear of the Lord is the
beginning of wisdom, and the knowledge
of the Holy One is understanding.

Proverbs 9:10

August 22

Let's deliberately aim to become more intimately acquainted with Christ. Not intimately acquainted with theology, as important as theology may be. Not intimately acquainted with the church, as valuable as the church may be. . . .

With Christ. With Him and Him alone! From this time forward, our goal in life is to become intimately acquainted with Him.

Seek first the kingdom
of God and His righteousness. . . .

Matthew 6:33, NKJV

August 23

We aren't just thrown on this earth like dice tossed across a table. We are sovereignly and lovingly placed here for a purpose.

God has given us a purpose for our existence, a reason to go on, even though that existence includes tough times. Living through suffering, we become sanctified—in other words, set apart for the glory of God. We gain perspective. We grow deeper. We grow up!

They cried out to the Lord
in their trouble; He saved them
out of their distresses.

Psalm 107:19

August 24

Those who are "born again" in the Lord Jesus Christ have been promised a living hope through His resurrection from the dead.

So if you want to smile through your tears, if you want to rejoice through times of suffering, just keep reminding yourself that, as a Christian, what you're going through isn't the end of the story . . . it's simply the rough journey that leads to the right destination.

How blessed are those
who keep justice, who practice
righteousness at all times.

Psalm 106:3

August 25

Two words will help you cope when you run low on hope: accept and trust.

Accept the mystery of hardship, suffering, misfortune, or mistreatment. Don't try to understand it or explain it. Accept it. Then, deliberately trust God to protect you by His power from this very moment to the dawning of eternity.

The Lord will be your confidence and will keep your foot from being caught.

Proverbs 3:26

August 26

Under heaven's lock and key, we are protected by the most efficient security system available—the power of God. There is no way we will be lost in the process of suffering. No disorder, no disease, not even death itself can weaken or threaten God's ultimate protection over our lives. No matter what the calamity, no matter what the disappointment or depth of pain, no matter what kind of destruction occurs in our bodies at the time of death, our souls are divinely protected.

We . . . are protected by the
power of God, through faith for a salvation
ready to be revealed in the last time.

1 Peter 1:5

AUGUST 27

We are commanded to stop (literally) . . . rest, relax, let go, and make time for God. The scene is one of stillness and quietness, listening and waiting before Him. Such foreign experiences in these busy times! Nevertheless, knowing God deeply and intimately requires such discipline. Silence is indispensable if we hope to add depth to our spiritual life.

Be still and
know that I am God.

PSALM 46:10, NIV

August 28

Paul had a thorn in the flesh, and he prayed three times for God to remove it. "No," said God, "I'm not taking it away." Finally Paul said, "I've learned to trust in You, Lord. I've learned to live with it." It was then God said, "My grace is sufficient for that thorn." He matched the color of the test with the color of grace.

My grace is sufficient for you,
for power is perfected in weakness.

2 Corinthians 12:9

August 29

Solitude is an oasis of the soul where we see ourselves, others, and especially our God in new ways. In solitude, struggles occur that no one else knows about. Inner battles are fought here that seldom become fodder for sermons or illustrations for books. God, who probes our deepest thoughts during protracted segments of solitude, opens our eyes to things that need attention. It is here He makes us aware of those things we try to hide from others.

When my anxious thoughts
multiply within me, your consolations
delight my soul.

Psalm 94:19

August 30

Anyone whose determined purpose is to become more deeply and intimately acquainted with God cannot retain the rights to his own position or place . . . or be anxiously preoccupied with working out the details of his own life. There must be complete and unqualified reliance on the Living Lord. In other words, one must develop the discipline of surrender.

My soul, wait in silence
for God only, for my hope
is from Him.

Psalm 62:5

August 31

God is fully trustworthy. I am finally learning this. I'm finally learning that His sovereign plan is the best plan. That whatever I entrust to Him, He can take care of better than I. That nothing under His control can ever be out of control. That everything I need, He knows about in every detail. That He is able to supply, to guide, to start, to stop, to sustain, to change, and to correct in His time and for His purposes. When I keep my hands out of things, His will is accomplished, His Name is exalted, and His glory is magnified.

May the Lord direct your hearts
into the love of God and into the
steadfastness of Christ.

2 Thessalonians 3:5

SEPTEMBER

A truly cheerful face comes from a joyful heart.

September 1

Perhaps this has been a difficult year for you. The future stretching out before you may seem gloomy or threatening. . . . In your rare moments of quiet, you may wonder, *Where is God?*

He's right there at your side, my friend. He has never left. He has never removed His eye from you, nor has His attention wandered to other matters. Not even for a heartbeat. He has never ceased caring for you, thinking about you, considering your situation, and loving you with a passion and intensity beyond comprehension.

My soul thirsts for God,
for the living God.

Psalm 42:2

September 2

God knows whether our noble acts and deeds are done out of pride and self-aggrandizement or whether they have been carried out in the power of the Spirit. He knows whether our inner, unseen thoughts and motives match our external words and works. He is pleased when our lives honor Him—inside and out. He is grieved when they do not.

Honor all people,
love the brotherhood, fear God,
honor the king.

1 Peter 2:17

September 3

Christ delivered us from slavery—slavery to a "futile way of life." Whether we knew it or not, we were trapped in a lifestyle that had only empty pleasures and dead-end desires to offer. We were in bondage to our impulses spawned from our sinful nature. In such a condition, we were hopelessly unable to help ourselves. The only way for us to be emancipated from that slavery was to have someone redeem us. That ransom price was paid by Christ, not with gold or silver, but with His precious blood.

Our old self was crucified
with Him . . . so that we would
no longer be slaves to sin.

Romans 6:6

September 4

Our eyes seem to be the closest connection to our minds. Through our eyes we bring in information and visual images. Through our eyes we feed our imaginations. Through our eyes we focus on things that are alluring and attractive and, don't kid yourself, extremely pleasurable for a while . . . *for a while.* Remember, the Bible says that Moses, by faith, gave up the "passing pleasures of sin" to walk with the people of God (Heb. 11:24–26). The cosmos offers pleasures, no doubt about it, but they are passing.

The wages of sin is death,
but the free gift of God is eternal life
in Christ Jesus our Lord.

Romans 6:23

September 5

It's easy to love Christ for all He is, for all He's done. It's not so easy, however, to love other Christians. Yet that is the command we have been given. . . .

If you want to make an impact on the world around you, this rugged society that is moving in the wrong direction more rapidly every year, He said, "love one another." That's how they'll know that you're different. Your love will speak with stunning eloquence to a lost world.

By this all men will know
that you are My disciples, if you
have love for one another.

John 13:35

September 6

God knows very well that His thoughts and ways infinitely surpass our own. He is mindful that He created us as finite beings out of a few pounds of garden soil. He understands that. He knows how to work with those limited in comprehension and frail of frame.

My question is, why don't *we* understand it? Why do we expect perfection of ourselves and of our associates?

He Himself knows
our frame; He is mindful
that we are but dust.

Psalm 103:14

September 7

You may truly sense that God has something for you to accomplish in a certain area. But if you aren't vigilant, if you aren't daily humbling yourself before Him, seeking His face, discerning His timing, operating under the Spirit's control, you may push and shove and force your way prematurely into that place where God wanted you, but you will not have arrived in His own time.

God waits for you to seek His counsel. If you act without discerning His timing, you may lose the smile of divine favor. He will not bless what He has not ordained.

We walk by faith,
not by sight.

2 Corinthians 5:7

September 8

Being obedient to the truth means that we don't have to look at others through the distorted lenses of our own biases. We can see them as God sees them and love them as He loves them. This has a purifying effect on us. It purges us, not only from a limited perspective, but from prejudice, resentment, hurt feelings, and grudges. Such purity of soul helps us love each other without hypocrisy and with a sincere love. It doesn't blind us to each other's faults; it gives us the grace to overlook them.

Love one another
fervently with a pure heart.

1 Peter 1:22, NKJV

September 9

In the human family, there are various kinds of birth experiences. But in God's family, everybody begins the same way. We are all adopted. We all have the same Father. We all come to Him the same way—through His Son, Jesus Christ. We are all members of the same family. Our backgrounds, our education, our social connections, our job, or how much money we have in the bank—all these things are irrelevant. We've all been born anew. We're all brothers and sisters in the Lord.

He predestined us to adoption
as sons through Jesus Christ to Himself,
according to the kind intention of His will.

Ephesians 1:5

September 10

What does He want for us this afternoon, tomorrow morning, or next week? Well, His plans for us are clearly set forth.

"I have plans for you, My son, My daughter," God says. "And they are great plans."

Each new dawn it's as if He smiles from heaven, saying, "Hope again . . . hope again!"

I know the plans that
I have for you, . . . plans for welfare
and not for calamity to give you
a future and a hope.

Jeremiah 29:11

September 11

Maybe, as you read these words, you're straining and kicking up lots of anxiety dust because life isn't moving rapidly enough; circumstances aren't changing at a fast enough clip.

I'm afraid I have some sad news for you. If that is your mindset, you will *always* be frustrated. Why? Because life will move along at its own pace. No matter how much you may will it to be so, circumstances will simply not conform themselves to your expectations or time schedule. If you try to force *events*, you will only give yourself blisters, ulcers, or an early heart attack.

He whose ear listens to the
life-giving reproof will dwell among the wise.

Proverbs 15:31

September 12

As never before in this generation, we realize that we are dependent upon God for protection and strength. Though the mountains quake, though bridges fall, though tunnels are destroyed, though ships sink, though lives will be lost, though war threatens to invade, though there may even be terrorists and enemies in our midst, we will not fear. Our resolve is firm because our refuge is based on the eternal foundation of the living God.

The firm foundation of
God stands, having this seal, "The Lord
knows those who are His."

2 Timothy 2:19

SEPTEMBER 13

Are you willing to be obscure? God will use failure in your life to break down that strong desire in your heart to see your name in lights. And when He finally breaks you of that lust for recognition, He may place you before the lights like you've never imagined. But then it won't matter. You won't care if you're prime time or small time, center stage or backstage, leading the charge or packing the baggage. You're just part of the King's army. People of selfless dedication are mainly . . . available. That's plenty!

Let us not become boastful,
challenging one another,
envying one another.

GALATIANS 5:26

September 14

Why does God lead us through desert places? That He might humble us, that He might test us, and that the true condition of our hearts might be revealed. Not that God might come to know you (He already does), but that *you* might come to know you. There's nothing like the desert to help you discover the real you. When you strip away all of the trappings, peel off all the masks, and shed all the phony costumes, you begin to see a true identity—a face that hasn't emerged for years. Maybe never.

Put on the new self, which in
the likeness of God has been created in
righteousness and holiness of the truth.

Ephesians 4:24

September 15

Contrary to popular opinion, God doesn't sit in heaven with His jaws clenched, His arms folded in disapproval, and a deep frown on His brow. He is not ticked off at His children for all the times we trip over our tiny feet and fall flat on our diapers. He is a loving Father, and we are precious in His sight, the delight of His heart. After all, He "has qualified us to share in the inheritance of the saints in light." Think of it! He's put us in His inheritance!

Giving thanks to the Father,
who has qualified us to share in the
inheritance of the saints in Light.

Colossians 1:12

September 16

God is for us. I want you to remember that.

God is for us. Say those four words to yourself.

God is for us.

Remember that tomorrow morning when you don't feel like He is. Remember that when you have failed. Remember that when you have sinned and guilt slams you to the mat.

God is for you.

Blessed be the Lord
your God who delighted in you. . . .

1 Kings 10:9

September 17

If the pace and the push, the noise and the crowds are getting to you, it's time to stop the nonsense and find a place of solace to refresh your spirit. Deliberately say "no" more often. This will leave room for you to slow down, get alone, pour out your overburdened heart, and admit your desperate need for inner refreshment. The good news is God will hear and He will help. The bad news is this: If you wait for someone else to bring about a change, things will only deteriorate.

As the deer pants for the water brooks,
So my soul pants for You, O God.

Psalm 42:1

September 18

God's plan doesn't require a drum roll or crashing cymbals. He doesn't use neon signs blinking, "Get ready! Get ready! Today's the day I do something big in your life."

That's not His style. God works by simply stepping into an ordinary day of life and saying what He wants to say. It's a meat-and-potatoes kind of proposition. Here's what needs doing, and you're the person who's going to do it, *so let's get after it!*

The Lord possessed me
at the beginning of His way,
before His works of old.

Proverbs 8:22

September 19

As you read these words, you may find yourself in a situation that seems terribly unfair. Your immediate circumstances are harsh and hard to handle. Your heart aches as events beyond your control roll across your landscape like heavy boulders. If that is your situation, I want you to take note: God knows, right down to the final nub, exactly where you are in life. He sees. He cares. He is aware. And best of all, He is touched by it.

I have surely seen the
affliction of My people . . . and have
given heed to their cry.

Exodus 3:7

SEPTEMBER 20

We didn't hunt Him down. He hunted us down. He is the eternal Hound of Heaven. We didn't work half our lives to find Him; He gave His life to find us! He is the Good Shepherd who gives His life for the sheep. When you find yourself slumping in shame or giving way to guilt, remind yourself of this: You have been chosen by the Good Shepherd. He wants you in His flock.

You did not
choose Me, but I chose you.

JOHN 15:16

September 21

No king has ever intimidated God, no matter how wealthy his treasury, how extensive his kingdom, or how powerful his armies. God can handle anyone. Anyone! He can handle your husband. He can handle your wife. He can handle your kids. . . . He can handle your ex-mate, that person who made you all those promises and broke most of them. He can even handle your enemy. He can handle the most intimidating situation, because in the hand of the Lord, any heart is like water.

The king's heart is like
channels of water in the hand of the Lord;
He turns it wherever He wishes.

Proverbs 21:1

September 22

We could call any work done in the will of God "the work of righteousness." And in doing that work, you will be surrounded by peace. Deep within you, in the very outworking of that service and that obedient walk, you will enjoy quietness and confidence. There will be an invincible sense of inner assurance, quietly and humbly accepted.

The work of righteousness
will be peace, and the service of righteousness,
quietness and confidence forever.

Isaiah 32:17

September 23

It may be that right now in your work you have come to an impasse; there's an issue of integrity at stake and you've determined not to compromise. Because of your stand for Christ, you find that you are resented. I want to assure you that if you handle that situation wisely and tactfully, God will see to it that in the eyes of those who are now your enemy, you will one day be esteemed. They will respect your stand because you are standing alone, doing what is right.

When a man's ways please
the LORD, He makes even his enemies
to be at peace with him.

PROVERBS 16:7, NKJV

September 24

You know the human response to panic? First, we are afraid. Second, we run. Third, we fight. Fourth, we tell everybody.

God's counsel is just the opposite. Don't be afraid. Stand still. Watch Him work. Keep quiet. It's then that He does it. He takes over! He handles it exactly opposite the way we'd do it. The Lord just taps His foot, waiting for us to wait.

Do not fear!
Stand by and see the salvation
of the Lord.

Exodus 14:13

September 25

God doesn't tell time as we do. Sometimes He does His work at three o' clock in the morning; sometimes at noon. He even works on Sundays. He does remarkable things, regardless of our time of day. . . . He ignores our deadlines and removes our crutches. He will leave our particular Red Sea absolutely closed, without an opening, without a sign, until He has finished teaching us the lessons we need to learn. Once that's accomplished, He has no trouble parting the waters and sending us through.

Splendor and majesty
are before Him; strength and
joy are in His place.

1 Chronicles 16:27

September 26

As a result of God's mercy, we have become a people who are uniquely and exclusively cared for by God. The fact that we are the recipients of His mercy makes all the difference in the world as to how we respond to difficult times. He watches over us with enormous interest. Why? Because of His immense mercy, freely demonstrated in spite of our not deserving it. What encouraging news!

Now you are the people of God;
you had not received mercy, but now
you have received mercy.

1 Peter 2:10

September 27

I'm convinced in my heart that if we were good students of submission we would get along a lot better in life. But I am also convinced that it is the one thing, more than any other, that works against our very natures, which argue, "I don't want to submit. I don't want to give in. I won't let him have his way in this." And so we live abrasively.

Let's get something very clear here. Our problem is not understanding what submission means. Our problem is doing what it says.

Teach me to do Your will,
for You are my God; let Your
good Spirit lead me.

Psalm 143:10

September 28

God puts us in the wilderness to test us, to stretch our spiritual muscles. Our earthly wilderness experiences are designed to develop us into men and women of faith. Let's face it, our spiritual roots grow deep only when the winds around us are strong. Take away the tests, and we become spiritual wimps. But bring on the wilderness winds, and it's remarkable how we grow, as our roots dig firmly into faith.

You shall remember all the way
which the Lord your God has led you . . .
that He might humble you.

Deuteronomy 8:2

September 29

It hurts to endure life's trials, and it hurts worse to repeat such episodes. Yet, without those deep hurts, we have very little capacity to receive godly counsel or make forward progress toward maturity.

Over the long haul, God is honing us through such tests. Stretching us. Breaking us. Crushing us. Reducing us to an absolute, open-armed trust, where we say, "Lord, I have come to the end of my own flesh."

The Lord also will be
a stronghold for the oppressed,
a stronghold in times of trouble.

Psalm 9:9

September 30

Some of us make grumbling a habit. Whether we're moving along in traffic or have been served a late meal, whether we're planning a last-minute arrangement with someone or working with a difficult group, we're given to complaining and grousing. It's like we have "the gift of grumbling" and feel we ought to exercise it, with gusto!

Are you prone to complaining? Remember, *God* is the one who has made your circumstances to be what they are. Don't blame someone else.

He has made
everything beautiful in its time.

Ecclesiastes 3:11, NKJV

OCTOBER

No one else is exactly like you. Refuse to compare or control.

October 1

Somewhere, miles away, crops push their way toward harvest and waves roar and tumble onto shore. Windswept forests sing their timeless songs, and desert animals scurry in the shadows of cactus and rock.

Within a matter of hours night will fall, the dark sky will glitter with moon and stars, and sleep will force itself upon us. Life will continue on uninterrupted. Appreciated or not, the canvas of nature will go on being painted by the fingers of God.

Be exalted, O God,
above the heavens, and Your glory
above all the earth.

Psalm 108:5

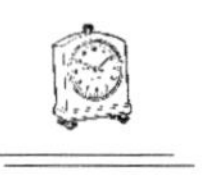

October 2

When you meet with God, open the Bible. Don't rely on your memory; rely on those printed pages.

Start at the beginning of a book of the Bible and work your way through it, slowly and systematically. Read it aloud. Read it thoughtfully. Listen to what your lips say and ask Him to make what you hear come alive in your life. Block out everything else. Pray it. Personalize it. Sing it. Make it a part of your conscious thought, and forget everything else as you give that time to Him.

O how I love Your law!
It is my meditation all the day.

Psalm 119:97

October 3

Do you have an uncaring boss? Do you have a supervisor or a manager who isn't fair? Do you have to deal with unreasonable people?

The natural tendency of the human heart is to fight back against unfair and unreasonable treatment. But seeking revenge for unjust suffering can be a sign of self-appointed lordship over one's own affairs. Revenge, then, is totally inappropriate for one who has submitted to the lordship of Jesus Christ.

Be submissive to your masters
with all respect, not only to those who are
good and gentle, but also to those
who are unreasonable.

1 Peter 2:18

October 4

Make a plan right now to keep a daily appointment with God. The enemy is going to tell you to set it aside, to do something else. He'll whisper, "You're far too involved with other things, far too busy." But every excuse he suggests is a lie.

If you're too busy to meet with the Lord, friend, then you are simply too busy. I repeat, you *must* carve out the time. Why not establish a plan before you go to bed tonight?

Let us come before
His presence with thanksgiving.

Psalm 95:2

October 5

The devil preys most greedily upon the godly. If you compromise your walk, you're not really a target of the enemy. Why should he waste his time? You're already halfway in his camp. But if you determine to stand alone and against the tide; if you determine to live according to biblical standards, be sure that your enemy is seeking to devour you.

But our great hope and assurance is that the One in us is greater than the one in the world.

Be self-controlled and alert.
Your enemy the devil prowls around
like a roaring lion.

1 Peter 5:8-9, NIV

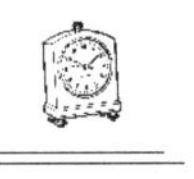

October 6

When you determine to be a person sold out to God—not just a run-of-the-mill, mediocre Christian accepting Christ as a fire escape—you become the object of God's special attention. He says He "sets you apart" for Himself. And the verse adds, "The Lord hears when I call to Him." Those two thoughts fit together. The godly often need to call upon God when the perils come. So He says, "I am here and I will answer. I will hear what you have to say."

The Lord has set apart
the godly man for himself; the Lord hears
when I call to Him.

Psalm 4:3

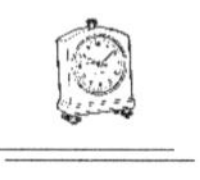

October 7

Has a friend betrayed you? . . . Has a disaster dropped on your life that's almost too great to bear? If so, don't fight back. Unjust suffering can be a dizzying experience. To keep your balance in those times when things are swirling around you, it's important to find a fixed reference point and focus on it. Return to the protection and guardianship of the Good Shepherd who endured the cross and laid down His life . . . for you.

I am the good shepherd;
the good shepherd lays down
His life for the sheep.

John 10:11

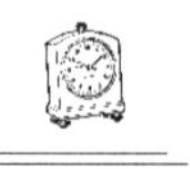

October 8

A wife is not responsible for her husband's life. She is responsible for her life. You cannot make your husband something he is not. Only God can do that.

I think it was the evangelist's wife, Ruth Graham, who once said, "It is my job to love Billy. It is God's job to make him good." I'd call that a wonderful philosophy for any wife to embrace.

He who has
My commandments and keeps them
is the one who loves Me.

John 14:21

October 9

You're not indispensable. I'm not indispensable. Nobody is indispensable, except the Lord Jesus Christ. He's the head. He's the Preeminent One. He's the founder. He's in first place. And when He moves one and brings in another or demotes one and sets up another, He calls the shots. That is His sovereign right. The problem arises when we get to thinking we're sovereign. My friend, He put you where He wanted you. He gave you that job. He can take it away just as fast as He gave it. Just faithfully do your work, lie low, and exalt Christ.

I in them and You in Me,
that they may be perfected in unity.

John 17:23

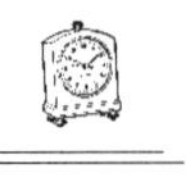

October 10

Wouldn't you love the ability to go back in time and change something you did or said?

But the sad fact is, we cannot go back. None of us can. We cannot undo sinful deeds or unsay sinful words. We cannot reclaim those moments when we were possessed by rage, or lust, or cruelty, or indifference, or hard-headed pride. We may be forgiven for those sins and have them blotted out of our record by the blood of Christ. Even so, we must live with the consequences of our words and our actions. What we sow, the Scriptures warn, we will also reap.

Whatever a man sows,
this he will also reap.

Galatians 6:7

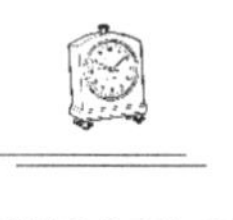

October 11

Only two things on earth are eternal: people and the Bible. When you're planning on retirement, don't plan on checking out with people or with God's Word. If you do, you'll be moving away from that which is eternal, and that's the wrong direction, my friend. So stay in touch. Give until you don't have anything else to give, and then tap into God's reservoirs and give some more. This is what lengthens the meaning and purpose—and sometimes the years—of life.

He will not often consider
the years of his life, because God keeps him
occupied with the gladness of his heart.

Ecclesiastes 5:20

October 12

God uses an infinite number of vehicles in the process of helping us grow. I do not know of any means that leads to instant growth. I've never met anyone who became instantly mature. It's a painstaking process that God takes us through, and it includes such things as waiting, failing, losing, and being misunderstood—each one calling for extra doses of perseverance.

Christian growth comes through hard-core, gutsy perseverance.

Apply your heart to discipline
and your ears to words of knowledge.

Proverbs 23:12

October 13

Want a challenge? Start modeling the truth . . . the whole truth and nothing but the truth, so help you God. Think truth. Confess truth. Face truth. Love truth. Pursue truth. Walk truth. Talk truth. Ah, that last one! That's a good place to begin. From this day forward, deliberately, consciously, and conscientiously speak the truth. Start practicing gut-level authenticity.

Give instruction
to a wise man and he will
be still wiser.

Proverbs 9:9

October 14

External beauty is ephemeral. Internal beauty is eternal. The former is attractive to the world; the latter is pleasing to God. Peter describes this inner beauty as "a gentle and quiet spirit." This might be paraphrased "a gentle tranquility." Without question, this is any woman's most powerful quality—true character. And such character comes from within—from the hidden person of the heart—because you know who you are and you know who you adore and serve, the Lord Christ.

Your adornment must not be
merely external . . . but let it be . . . a gentle
and quiet spirit, which is precious
in the sight of God.

1 Peter 3:3–4

October 15

God's goal for us as husbands is to be sensitive rather than to prove how strong and macho we are. We need to love our wives, listen to them, adapt to their needs. We need to say no to more and more in our work so we can say yes to more and more in our homes . . . so we can say yes to the needs of our children and our families. (How else will your children learn what it means to be a good husband and father?)

The merciful man
does himself good.

Proverbs 11:17

October 16

Believers who are growing toward maturity share in mutual feelings—mutual woes and mutual joys.

This is one of the best benefits of being part of the body of Christ and a major reason why we need to be involved in a local church. In that local community we have a context in which we can rejoice with each other and weep with one another.

Rejoice with those
who rejoice, and weep with
those who weep.

Romans 12:15

October 17

As a good shepherd, Jesus looked at humanity's lost sheep who were scattered, frightened, and hungry. What He saw pulled at His heartstrings. He was full of tenderness for them. He had compassion for them. Just as these hurting people touched the heart of the Savior, so should hurting people today touch our hearts.

When He saw the multitudes,
He was moved with compassion for them,
because they were weary and scattered,
like sheep having no shepherd.

Matthew 9:36, NKJV

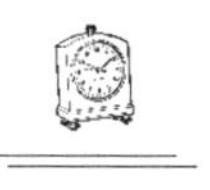

October 18

Some of the best times in prayer are wordless times. I stop speaking, close my eyes, and meditate upon what I have been reading or upon what I have been saying, and I listen inside of myself. I listen deeply. I listen for reproofs. . . . It is here that the Holy Spirit invades.

Please be assured that I have never heard an audible voice. It isn't that kind of answering. It's a listening down inside. It's sensing what God is saying about the situation. His promise is, after all, that He will inscribe His law—His will—upon our hearts and our minds.

My soul waits
in silence for God only.

Psalm 62:1

October 19

To love and to be loved is the bedrock of our existence. But love must also flex and adapt. Rigid love is not true love. It is veiled manipulation, a conditional time bomb that explodes when frustrated. Genuine love willingly waits! It isn't pushy or demanding. While it has its limits, its boundaries are far-reaching. It neither clutches nor clings. Real love is not shortsighted, selfish, or insensitive. It detects needs and does what is best for the other person without being told.

Love is patient, love is kind.

1 Corinthians. 13:4

October 20

We know the sovereign Potter is working with us as He pleases. He is the Potter, we are the clay. He is the one who gives the commands; we are the ones who obey. He never has to explain Himself; He never has to ask permission. He is shaping us over into the image of His Son, regardless of the pain and heartache that may require. Those lessons are learned a little easier when we remember that we are not in charge, He is.

You are our Father,
we are the clay, and You our potter; and all
of us are the work of Your hand.

Isaiah 64:8

October 21

Take from us our wealth and we are hindered. Take our health and we are handicapped. Take our purpose and we are slowed, temporarily confused. But take away our hope and we are plunged into deepest darkness . . . stopped dead in our tracks, paralyzed. Wondering, "Why?" Asking, "How much longer? Will this darkness ever end? Does God know where I am?"

Then the Father says, "That's far enough," and how sweet it is! Hope revives and washes over us.

He who dwells in the shelter
of the Most High will abide in the
shadow of the Almighty.

Psalm 91:1

October 22

If you are blessed with abilities, if you are gifted, if you are used by God, it is easy to start believing your own stuff. Yet one of the marks of a truly mature life is humility of spirit.

A truly humble person looks for opportunities to give himself freely to others rather than holding back, to release rather than hoarding, to build up rather than tearing down, to serve rather than being served, to learn from others rather than clamoring for the teaching stand. How blessed are those who learn this early in life.

He who pursues righteousness
and loyalty finds life, righteousness,
and honor.

Proverbs 21:21

October 23

God misses nothing. He's looking out for us. He's listening to our prayers. And He is completely aware of the evil that is happening to us.

Don't ever think He has missed the evil. He sees, and He remembers. He may be long-suffering, but He doesn't compromise His justice. Not only is His eye on the righteous, His face is against evil. Ultimately, good will overcome evil. In the end, God wins!

The eyes of the Lord
are toward the righteous, and His ears
attend to their prayer.

1 Peter 3:12

October 24

Jesus came to serve and to give. It makes sense, then, to say that God desires the same for us. After bringing us into His family through faith in His Son, the Lord God sets His sights on building into us the same quality that made Jesus distinct from all others in His day. He is engaged in building into His people the same serving and giving qualities that characterized His Son.

The Son of Man
did not come to be served,
but to serve.

Mark 10:45

October 25

The Pharisees, were great on loud, dogmatic commands, lengthy requirements, and drawn-out demands. Oh, how they loved the sound of their own words! But when it came to doing, they struck out.

James exhorts us to be "doers of the word, and not merely hearers." In other words, don't talk compassion; lend a hand. Don't pound a pulpit about generosity; give. Just do it.

Prove yourselves
doers of the word, and not
merely hearers.

James 1:22

October 26

Stop permitting two strong tendencies—selfishness and conceit—to control you! Let nothing either of them suggests win a hearing. Replace them with "humility of mind." But how? By regarding others as more important than yourself. Look for ways to support, encourage, build up, and stimulate the other person. And that requires an attitude that would rather give than receive.

With humility of mind
regard one another as more important
than yourselves.

Philippians 2:3

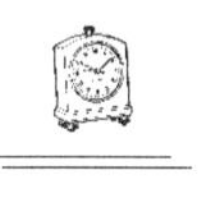

October 27

It defies the human mind to find the depths of the mind of God. A scholar may spend years studying another human being—his life, his writings, his work—and ultimately have a deep understanding of that person. We can plumb the depths of another's mind. But we cannot begin to scratch the surface of the unsearchable judgments of God.

How unsearchable are His judgments
and unfathomable His ways. For who has
known the mind of the Lord.

Romans 11:33–34

October 28

There is only one you. You're the only person with your exact heritage, your precise series of events in the pilgrimage and sufferings of life that have brought you to this hour. You're the only one with your personal convictions, your makeup, your skills, your appearance, your touch, your voice, your style, your surroundings, your sphere of influence—you're the only one.

You have granted me life
and lovingkindness; and Your care
has preserved my spirit.

Job 10:12

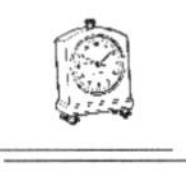

October 29

When you persevere through a trial, God gives you a special measure of insight. You become the recipient of the favor of God as He gives to you, and those who suffer with you, something that would not be learned otherwise.

He will redeem
my soul in peace from the battle
which is against me.

Psalm 55:18

October 30

Is there something you are waiting for, something you are trusting God to do, to perform, to fulfill, and He hasn't done it yet? You are probably waiting longer than you thought you would have to wait. But that doesn't mean God's provision is canceled, it just means His promise is delayed. Our timetable is different from His, and on occasion He will say, "Wait." I repeat, the delay doesn't mean He has canceled it, it simply means He's building our character through the process of waiting.

I waited patiently for the Lord;
and He inclined to me and heard my cry.

Psalm 40:1

October 31

When you're hungry and weary and thirsty in the wilderness, that's when a friend comes through. You don't even have to ask. When you've got a friend like this, he knows you're hungry. He knows you're thirsty. He knows you're weary. The beautiful thing about sheltering friends is that they don't have to be told what to do . . . the practical stuff. They just do it. This is faith in action.

A friend loves at all times.

Proverbs 17:17

NOVEMBER

When Christ becomes our focus, contentment replaces anxiety.

November 1

Get your "stuff" together. Act like a man. Be brave and courageous as a lady. You're the only one on the sales force who's telling the truth? Good for you! Keep it up. God honors integrity, which is another sign of maturity. When other people are responsible for good things happening, always give them the credit. That's what mature adults do. Servant-hearted leadership is wonderful to behold.

Be on the alert,
stand firm in the faith, . . . be strong.

1 Corinthians 16:13

NOVEMBER 2

If we will only believe and ask, a full measure of God's grace and peace is available to any of us. By the wonderful, prevailing mercy of God, we can find purpose in the scattering and sadness of our lives. We can not only deal with suffering but rejoice through it. Though our pain and our disappointment and the details of our suffering may differ, there is an abundance of God's grace and peace available to each one of us.

All things you ask in prayer,
believing, you will receive.

MATTHEW 21:22

November 3

When we are suffering, only Christ's perspective can replace our resentment with rejoicing. I've seen it happen in hospital rooms. I've seen it happen in families. I've seen it happen in my own life.

Our whole perspective changes when we catch a glimpse of the purpose of Christ in it all. Take that away, and it's nothing more than a bitter, terrible experience.

Come to Me, all who are weary
and heavy-laden, and I will give you rest.

Matthew 11:28

NOVEMBER 4

The Lord is our God. He does not bow to our hurried pace, but in silence He waits for us to meet His demands. And once we slow down enough to meet Him, He is pleased to add incredible spiritual depth to our shallow lives.

From the rising of the sun to its setting
the name of the LORD is to be praised.

PSALM 113:3

NOVEMBER 5

Almost every day—certainly every week—we encounter people who are in their own homemade boat, thinking seriously about setting forth. The ocean of possibilities is enormously inviting, yet terribly threatening. Urge them on! Dare to say what they need to hear the most, "Go for it!" Then pray like mad. How much could be accomplished if only there were more brave souls on the end of the pier smiling and affirming.

Surely there is a future,
and your hope will not
be cut off.

PROVERBS 23:18

November 6

As one understanding soul expressed it: "Compassion is not a snob gone slumming. It's a real trip down inside the broken heart of a friend."

Parceling out this kind of compassion will elicit no whistles or loud applause. In fact, the best acts of compassion will never be known to the masses. Nor will fat sums of money be dumped into your lap because you are committed to being helpful. Normally, acts of mercy are done in obscurity with no thought (or receipt) of monetary gain.

Dispense true justice and
practice kindness and compassion
each to his brother.

Zechariah 7:9

NOVEMBER 7

God's redemptive providence is always at work, even through the most diabolical schemes and actions. . . .

So, take heart, my friend. God is in full control. Nothing is happening on earth that brings a surprise to heaven. Nothing is outside the scope of His divine radar screen as He guides us safely home. Things that seem altogether confusing, without reason, unfair, even wrong, do indeed fit into the Father's providential plan.

Now to the King eternal,
immortal, invisible, the only God, be honor
and glory forever and ever.

1 TIMOTHY 1:17

November 8

Jesus Christ met people where they were . . . not as they "ought to" be. Angry young men, blind beggars, proud politicians, loose-living streetwalkers, ignorant fishermen, naked victims of demonism, and grieving parents were as clearly in His focus as the Twelve who sometimes hung on His every word.

His enemies misunderstood Him, but they couldn't ignore Him. They hated Him, but were never bored around Him. Jesus was the epitome of relevance. Still is.

I will put My laws into their minds,
and I will write them on their hearts.
And I will be their God.

Hebrews 8:10

November 9

The simple fact is this: If we sow a lifestyle that is in direct disobedience to God's revealed Word, we ultimately reap disaster.

The consequences of sin may not come immediately . . . but they will come eventually. And when they do, there will be no excuses, no rationalization, no accommodation. God doesn't compromise with consequences. When the bill comes due, the wages of willful sin must be paid in full.

Shall we sin because we are
not under law but under grace?
May it never be!

Romans 6:15

November 10

An advocate is someone who has authority, someone who will be heard and respected, where we would be ignored. The more passionate and complicated the issue, the more vital is our need for a qualified go-between. . . .

There is one Advocate we all need—one who represents sinners like us in the highest of all places—the presence of God: "Jesus Christ the righteous." What a great promise!

If anyone sins,
we have an Advocate with the Father,
Jesus Christ the righteous.

1 John 2:1

November 11

Our trials are not superficial or irrelevant. They are vehicles of grace that God uses to bring us growth. Superficial problems call for superficial solutions. But real life isn't like that; its headaches and stresses go deeper, right down to the bone. They touch the nerve areas of our security. But God says He is a present help in trouble. He is immediately available. Do you realize that wherever you travel, whatever the time of day, you can call and He will answer?

Call to Me and I will answer you,
and I will tell you great and mighty things,
which you do not know.

Jeremiah 33:3

NOVEMBER 12

Our Lord is intimately acquainted with all our ways. Darkness and light are alike to Him. Not one of us is hidden from His sight. All things are open and laid bare before Him: our darkest secret, our deepest shame, our stormy past, our worst thought, our hidden motive, our vilest imagination . . . even our vain attempts to cover the ugly with snow-white beauty.

He comes up so close. He sees it all. He knows our frame. He remembers we are dust. . . . Best of all, He loves us still.

Love covers
all transgressions.

PROVERBS 10:12

NOVEMBER 13

Close your eyes for a moment. I want you to think about what seems most impossible. Nothing is impossible with God. Is it your business? Or your school? Or your marriage? How about keeping the house clean, keeping up with the wash, having a ministry with others, or healing strained relationships with people? Will you ask the Lord to handle that specific impossibility, and then leave it with Him in a faith that simply will not doubt?

Nothing is too difficult for You.

JEREMIAH 32:17

November 14

It is helpful to remember the distinction between appreciation and affirmation. We appreciate what a person *does*, but we affirm who a person *is*. Appreciation comes and goes because it is usually related to something someone accomplishes. Affirmation goes deeper. It is directed to the person himself or herself. While encouragement would encompass both, the rarer of the two is affirmation.

All of us need encouragement—somebody to believe in us.

Good understanding produces favor.

Proverbs 13:15

November 15

Compassion usually calls for a willingness to humbly spend oneself in obscurity on behalf of unknowns. . . . Truly compassionate people are often hard to understand. They take risks most people would never take. They give away what most people would cling to. They reach out and touch when most would hold back with folded arms. Their caring brings them up close where they feel the other person's pain and do whatever is necessary to demonstrate true concern.

It is better to be humble
in spirit with the lowly than to divide
the spoil with the proud.

Proverbs 16:19

November 16

God would love to piece together the shattered fragments of your life. But He is waiting . . . graciously waiting until the time is right.

Until you are tired of the life you are living . . . until you see it for what it really is.

Until you are weary of coping . . . of taking charge of your own life . . . until you realize the mess you are making of it.

Until you recognize your need for Him. . . . He's waiting.

How delightful
is a timely word!

Proverbs 15:23

November 17

Personally, I think a healthy sense of humor is determined by at least three abilities:

The ability to laugh at our own mistakes.

The ability to accept justified criticism—and get over it!

The ability to interject (or at least enjoy) wholesome humor when surrounded by a tense, heated situation.

A joyful heart
makes a cheerful face.

Proverbs 15:13

November 18

If there were one great message I could deliver to those who struggle with not having an abundance of this world's goods, it would be this simple yet profound premise for happiness: Great wealth is not related to money! It is an attitude of satisfaction coupled with inner peace, plus a day-by-day, moment-by-moment walk with God. Sounds so right, so good, doesn't it? In our world of more, more, more . . . push, push, push . . . grab, grab, grab, this counsel is long overdue. In a word, the secret is contentment.

Better is a little with
righteousness than great income
with injustice.

Proverbs 16:8

November 19

Thanks to the Word of God, we can list several marks of integrity that God would have us appropriate into our lives. Do you have these marks of integrity?

An excellent attitude

Faithfulness and diligence at work

Personal purity of the highest caliber

Consistency in your walk with God

Self-examination is up to you. It is not only a good idea, it's a biblical imperative.

If we judged ourselves rightly,
we would not be judged.

1 Corinthians 11:31

November 20

Three things are required for spiritual victory: birth, faith, and truth. In order to enter into the ranks of the victorious, we must be "born of God." It occurs when I accept Jesus Christ as savior.

Then comes faith. I draw upon the power that is in me. I no longer operate on the basis of human strength, but by faith. I rely upon divine power.

Then truth. Everything is made possible by the truth, by believing the truth, by living the truth.

You will know the truth,
and the truth will make you free.

John 8:32

November 21

Memories . . .

Want to have something meaningful to look back on for the rest of your life? Want a scrapbook of scattered pictures filled with smiling faces? Do yourself and your family a favor. Paint some watercolor memories together this summer . . . or fall . . . or winter . . . or spring.

People who do that are not just sentimental . . . they're smart.

Bless the LORD, O my soul,
and forget none of His benefits.

Psalm 103:1

November 22

You do not have to pay the price to grow and expand intellectually. The mind neither requires it nor demands it. If, however, you want to experience the joy of discovery and the pleasure of plowing new and fertile soil, effort is required.

Light won't automatically shine upon you, nor will truth silently seep into your head by means of rocking-chair osmosis. . . . It's up to you. It's your move.

The mind of man plans his way,
but the LORD directs his steps.

Proverbs 16:9

November 23

Periodically, we will find ourselves at a loss to know what to do or how to respond. It's then we ask for help, and God delivers more than intelligence and ideas and good old common sense. He dips into His well of wisdom and allows us to drink from His bucket, whose refreshment provides abilities and insights that are of another world. Perhaps it might best be stated as having a small portion of "the mind of Christ."

If any of you
lacks wisdom let him ask of God,
who gives to all generously.

James 1:5, NASB

November 24

After enduring the bitterness of winter, the early colonists decided to hold a feast, celebrating their survival and giving thanks to God for His protection and provisions throughout the past months. It was a spontaneous celebration of praise. God had turned their hardship and sorrow and pain into gratitude and health and joy.

Praise the LORD, all nations;
laud Him, all peoples! For His lovingkindness
is great toward us.

Psalm 117:1–2

November 25

We need to lock onto the power that comes from God's presence and invite Him to cleanse our thoughts, to correct our foul speech, to forgive us completely, and make us holy vessels who, like those winged seraphim, spend our days bringing glory to His holy name.

Take a really honest look at your walk. Are there any areas where old sins have begun to take control again? This would be a wonderful time to allow Him to bring fresh order out of longstanding chaos.

Let the words of my mouth
and the meditation of my heart be
acceptable in Your sight.

Psalm 19:14

November 26

In a world consumed with thoughts of itself, filled with people impressed with each other, having disconnected with the only One worthy of praise, it's time we return to Theology 101 and sit silently in His presence. It's time we catch a fresh glimpse of Him who, alone, is awesome. He is our infinite, inexhaustible God. Any serious study of Him takes us from an unconscious to conscious awareness of our ignorance.

The One we worship defies human analysis.

Our God is in the heavens;
He does whatever He pleases.

Psalm 115:3

November 27

At this moment you may be experiencing tremendous prosperity in your business or your personal life. You may find yourself coasting along, and it looks like a beautiful tomorrow. If so, let me challenge you: Right now you are in the perfect place to prepare yourself. Times of peace and prosperity provide the ideal moments to equip yourself for the inevitable tests of famine and hardship.

I have directed you
in the way of wisdom; I have led
you in upright paths.

Proverbs 4:11

November 28

This may shock you, but I believe the single most significant decision I can make on a day-to-day basis is my choice of attitude. It is more important than my past, my education, my bankroll, my successes or failures, fame or pain, what other people think of me, or say about me, my circumstances, or my position. The attitude I choose keeps me going or cripples my progress. When my attitudes are right, there's no barrier too high, no valley too deep.

Keep sound wisdom and discretion. . . .
Then you will walk in your way securely,
and your foot will not stumble.

Proverbs 3: 21, 23

November 29

Think it over. Are you living every day as if it's your last for His glory? Do you work diligently at your job and in your home (as if He isn't coming for another ten years) for His name's sake?

Do you shake salt and shine the light every chance you get?

Do you remain balanced, cheerful, winsome, and stable, anticipating His return?

The Lord Himself will descend
from heaven with a shout, . . . and the
dead in Christ shall rise first.

1 Thessalonians 4:16

November 30

When you face an impossibility, leave it in the hands of the Specialist! Refuse to calculate. Refuse to doubt. Refuse to work it out by yourself. Refuse to worry.

Instead, say, "Lord, I'm carrying around something I cannot handle. Because You are not only able but also willing, take this off my hands. It's impossible to me, but is as nothing with You." Persevering through the pressures of impossibilities calls for that kind of confidence.

I will not forget you!
See, I have engraved you on
the palms of my hands.

Isaiah 49:16, NIV

DECEMBER

Let's choose each day
to keep an attitude of faith and joy
and belief and compassion.

December 1

Nobody is a whole chain. Each one is a link. But take away one link and the chain is broken.

Nobody is a whole team. Each one is a player. But take away one player and the game is forfeited.

Nobody is a whole orchestra. Each one is a musician. But take away one musician and the symphony is incomplete.

We need each other. You need someone and someone needs you. Isolated islands, we're not.

We have not ceased to pray for you; . . .
that you will walk in a manner worthy of the Lord.

Colossians 1:9

December 2

I have discovered that a joyful countenance has nothing to do with one's age or one's occupation (or lack of it) or one's geography or education or marital status or good looks or circumstances. Joy is a choice!

Joy is a matter of attitude that stems from one's confidence in God—that He is at work, that He is in full control, that He is in the midst of whatever has happened, is happening, and will happen.

You have put
gladness in my heart.

Psalm 4:7

DECEMBER 3

God allows suffering so that we might learn what it means to depend on Him. Over and over He reminds us of the danger of pride, but it frequently takes suffering to make the lesson stick.

God also allows suffering so that we might learn to give thanks in everything. Now, honestly, have you said, "Thanks, Lord, for this test"? Have you finally stopped struggling and expressed to Him how much you appreciate His loving sovereignty over your life?

Though a host encamp
against me, my heart will not fear; . . .
I shall be confident.

PSALM 27:3

December 4

When money is our objective for happiness, we must live in fear of losing it, which makes us paranoid and suspicious. When fame is our aim, we become competitive lest others upstage us, which makes us envious. When power and influence drive us, we become self-serving and strong-willed, which makes us arrogant. And when possessions become our god, we become materialistic, thinking enough is never enough, which makes us greedy. All these pursuits fly in the face of contentment and joy.

For to me, living means
opportunities for Christ, and dying—
well, that's better yet!

Philippians 1:21, TLB

December 5

There are many voices these days. Some are loud, many are persuasive, and a few are downright convincing. It can be confusing. If you listen long enough you will be tempted to throw your faith to the winds, look out for number one, let your glands be your guide, and choose what is best for you. Initially you will get a rush of pleasure and satisfaction, no question. But ultimately you will wind up disappointed and disillusioned.

It is better to
take refuge in the LORD than
to trust in a man.

PSALM 118:8

December 6

To be humble in heart . . . is to be submissive to the core. It involves being more interested in serving the needs of others than in having one's own needs met.

Someone who is truly unselfish is generous with his or her time and possessions, energy and money. As that works its way out, it is demonstrated in various ways, such as thoughtfulness and gentleness, an unpretentious spirit, and servant-hearted leadership.

With humility of mind
regard one another as more important
than yourselves.

Philippians 2:3

December 7

Are you an eagle-type, soaring high beyond your peers? Do you find yourself bored with the maintenance of the machinery . . . yawning through the review of the rules . . . restless to cut a new swath . . . excited rather than intimidated by the risks? If so, don't expect pats on the back or great waves of applause. Chances are you may even lose a few jobs, fail a few courses, and ruffle tons of feathers. Mavericks who don't color within the lines are also notorious for not staying within the fences. And that makes folks terribly uncomfortable.

But take heart! You're in good company!

The ways of a man are before the
eyes of the Lord, and He watches all his paths.

Proverbs 5:21

December 8

Contrary to popular opinion, work is not the result of the curse. Adam was given the task of cultivating and keeping the Garden before sin ever entered (Gen. 2:15).

Then what was the curse? It was the addition of "thorns and thistles" that turned work into a "toil" and made the whole thing a sweaty hassle. But work itself is a privilege, a high calling, a God-appointed assignment to be carried out for His greater glory.

There is precious treasure
and oil in the dwelling of the wise.

Proverbs 21:20

December 9

I like the word *gumption* because it's so homely and so forlorn and so out of style it looks as if it needs a friend and isn't likely to reject anyone who comes along. It's an old Scottish word, once used a lot by pioneers, but . . . seems to have all but dropped out of use.

A person filled with gumption doesn't sit around, dissipating and stewing about things. He's at the front of the train of his own awareness, watching to see what's up the track and meeting it when it comes.

O Lord, lead me in
your righteousness; . . . make Your way
straight before me.

Psalm 5:8

December 10

I'm comforted when I realize that God is in sovereign control of all of life. He not only knows the times and the seasons; He is also Lord of the unexpected and the unpredictable. Our times and our trials are in His hands. Even when we feel embarrassed or confused or do something really weird.

Whether we're on cloud nine, enjoying His blessings, or caught in the thicket of some tangled predicament, He hasn't let us go. By His grace, He remains "for us."

If God is for us,
who is against us?

Romans 8:31

December 11

The average life span may be seventy-five to eighty years, but who can say you or I have that long? We may have less than two years or, for that matter, less than two weeks.

Since this is true, let's do our best to make the time we have count. Rather than live with reluctance, let's live with exuberance. Instead of fearing what's ahead, let's face it head-on with enthusiasm. And because life is so terribly short, let's do everything we can to make it sweet.

You are just a vapor that appears
for a little while and then vanishes away,

James 4:14

December 12

I know human nature well enough to realize that some people excuse their bitterness over past hurts by thinking: "It's too late to change. I've been injured and the wrong done against me is too great for me ever to forget it." A person with this mind-set is convinced that he or she is the exception to the command to forgive and is determined not to change.

But when God holds out hope, when God makes promises, there are no exceptions.

I hope in You, O Lord;
You will answer, O Lord my God.

Psalm 38:15

December 13

The Pharisees hated Jesus because He refused to let them get away with their phony religious drool!

If there was one thing Jesus despised, it was the very thing every Pharisee majored in at seminary: showing off. Another word for it is "self-righteousness." The Messiah unsheathed His sharp sword of truth . . . exposing their pride. Like never before, the smug show-offs were put in their place!

Beware of practicing
your righteousness before men
to be noticed by them.

Matthew 6:1

December 14

The two most important tools of parenting are time and touch. Believe me, both are essential. If you and I hope to release from our nest fairly capable and relatively stable people who can soar and make it on their own, we'll need to pay the price of saying no to many of our own wants and needs in order to interact with our young. . . . And we'll have to keep breaking down the distance that only naturally forms as our little people grow up.

Time and touch. Listen to your boys and girls, look them in the eye, put your arms around them, hug them close, tell them how valuable they are.

A righteous man who walks in his integrity—
how blessed are his sons after him.

Proverbs 20:7

December 15

I honestly believe that "forgetting" is the hardest part of "forgiving." Forgetting is something shared with no other person. It's a solo flight. And all the rewards are postponed until eternity . . . but how great they will be on that day! Forgetting requires the servant to think correctly, which means our full focus must be on the Lord and not on humanity. By God's grace, it can happen.

Greater is he who is in you
than he who is in the world.

1 John 4:4

December 16

The Christian life boils down to a battle of the wills: Christ's vs. our own. Every day we live we must answer, "Who's in charge here?"

Recently I received a letter from a fine Christian couple, and I smiled understandingly at one line: "Although the Lord has taken good care of my wife and me for the past thirty-eight years, He has taken control of us for the past two and a half."

Tell me, how long has the Lord taken care of you? Be honest now . . . has He also taken control of you?

What is man that
You take thought of him?

Psalm 8:4

December 17

Character threads don't "suddenly" snap. As the British expositor of yesteryear, F. B. Meyer, once put it, "No man suddenly becomes base."

Slowly, silently, subtly, things are tolerated that once were rejected. At the outset everything appears harmless, maybe even a bit exciting. But with it comes an "insignificant" wedge, a gap that grows wider as moral erosion joins hands with spiritual decay.

Be on guard!

There is a way which
seems right to a man, but its end
is the way of death.

Proverbs 14:12

December 18

There's nothing like crisis to expose the otherwise hidden truth of the soul. Any soul.

Remember Alexander Solzhenitzyn's admission? "It was only when I lay there on rotting prison straw that I sensed within myself the first stirrings of good. . . . So bless you, prison, for having been in my life."

Take away the cushion of comfort, remove the shield of safety, interject the threat of death . . . and it's fairly certain most in the ranks of humanity commence prayer.

Before I was afflicted I went astray,
but now I obey your word.

Psalm 119:67, NIV

December 19

With each new dawn there is delivered to your door a fresh, new package called "today." God has designed each of us in such a way that we can handle only one package at a time . . . and all the grace we need will be supplied by Him as we live out that day.

Those who know
Your name will put their trust in You,
for You, O Lord, have not forsaken
those who seek You.

Psalm 9:10

December 20

Being cordial literally starts from the heart, as I see it. It begins with the deep-seated belief that the other person is important, genuinely significant, deserving of my undivided attention, my unrivaled interest, if only for a few seconds. Encouraged by such a belief, I am prompted to be sensitive to that person's feelings. If he is uneasy and self-conscious, cordiality alerts me to put him at ease. If she is shy, cordiality provides a relief. If he is bored, cordiality stimulates and invigorates him. If she is sad, cordiality brings cheer. What a needed and necessary virtue it is!

Put on love, which is
the perfect bond of unity.

Colossians 3:14

December 21

If you know someone is a real pro at chess, take my advice: Don't waste your time playing against him. You can't win! Nobody knows this better than the devil. He's playing against a pro, and he knows it. He keeps making his moves, but he's already been defeated. So if you want to defeat the devil, you will not do it in the strength of the flesh; you'll do it in the power of the Lord Jesus Christ. His blood will overcome and render powerless the power of the devil.

He rescued us from the domain
of darkness, and transferred us to the
kingdom of His beloved Son.

Colossians 1:13

December 22

There is Someone who fully knows what lurks in our hearts. And knowing, He never laughs mockingly and fades away. He never shrugs and walks away. Instead, He understands completely and stays near.

Who, indeed, knows? Our God, alone knows. He sympathizes with our weaknesses and forgives all our transgressions. To Him there are no secret struggles or silent cries. He hears. He sees. He stays near.

The Lord is near
to all who call upon Him.

Psalm 145:18

December 23

If we would ask more, we would have more. But because we don't ask, we don't have. I wonder how many wonderful gifts are left wrapped in heaven because they were never asked to be unwrapped on earth? They just remained there, unasked for.

You do not have
because you do not ask.

James 4:2

December 24

When it came time for God to send His Son to earth, He did not send Him to the palace of some mighty king. He was conceived in the womb of an unwed mother—a virgin!—who lived in the lowly village of Nazareth.

In choosing those who would represent Christ and establish His church, God picked some of the most unusual individuals imaginable: unschooled fishermen, a tax collector(!), a mystic, a doubter, and a former Pharisee who had persecuted Christians. He continued to pick some very unusual persons down through the ages. In fact, He seems to delight in such surprising choices to this very day.

He has . . . exalted those who were humble.

Luke 1:52

December 25

As the year draws to a close, Christmas offers its wonderful message: Emmanuel. God with us. He who resided in Heaven, co-equal and co-eternal with the Father and the Spirit, willingly descended into our world. He breathed our air, felt our pain, knew our sorrows, and died for our sins. He didn't come to frighten us, but to show us the way to warmth and safety.

Blessed be the Lord God of Israel,
for He has visited us and accomplished
redemption for His people.

Luke 1:68

December 26

Pearls are the products of irritation. This irritation occurs when the shell of the oyster is invaded by an alien substance like a grain of sand. When that happens, all the resources within the tiny, sensitive oyster rush to the irritated spot and begin to release healing fluids. . . . By and by the irritant is covered—by a pearl. Had there been no irritating interruption, there could have been no pearl.

No wonder our heavenly home has pearly gates to welcome the wounded and bruised.

The refining pot is for silver and
the furnace for gold, but the Lord tests hearts.

Proverbs 17:3

December 27

God has entrusted to us a great deal. He knows that we can do all things by His grace, so He's trusting in us to trust in Him. Yet He knows our fears as well, otherwise He wouldn't assure us so often of His purposes and His presence.

We feel hurt and alone, God assures us He cares.

We feel angry and resentful, God provides wisdom and strength.

We feel ashamed, God grants forgiveness and comfort.

We feel anxious, God promises to supply all our needs.

You have seen my affliction;
you have known the troubles of my soul.

Psalm 31:7

December 28

A number of years ago, I heard a Chinese man say, after going through two terrible wars and losing every member of his family, that he had come to realize his best times with God were early in the morning. In fact, he said, "I live by the motto: No Bible, no Breakfast." I don't remember anything else he said aside from his circumstances and that statement.

Make me understand
the way of Your precepts, so I will
meditate on Your wonders.

Psalm 119:27

December 29

The difference between something good and something great is attention to detail. That is true of a delicious meal, a musical presentation, a play, a clean automobile, a well-kept home, a church, our attire, a business, a lovely garden, a sermon, a teacher, a well-disciplined family.

Let's make a long-term commitment to quality control. Let's move out of the thick ranks of the mediocre and join the thin ranks of excellence.

I'm ready if you are.

I have seen that nothing
is better than that man should be happy
in his activities, for that is his lot.

Ecclesiastes 3:22

December 30

Jesus mastered the art of maintaining a clear perspective while accomplishing every single one of His objectives. Though we never read of His hurrying anywhere, He managed to fulfill the complete agenda. Just before the agony of the cross, He told the Father that He had "finished the work which You have given Me to do" (John 17:4, NKJV). And only seconds before He drew His last breath, He made that epochal statement, "It is finished" (John 19:30). Nothing essential was left undone.

The path of the righteous is like
the light of dawn, that shines brighter and
brighter until the full day.

Proverbs 4:18

December 31

We are only finite human beings. We can only see the present and the past. The future is a little frightening to us. So we need to hold onto God's hand and trust Him to calm our fears. And at those times when we're stubborn and resisting and He shakes us by the shoulders to get our attention, we're reminded that we don't call the shots. God has a plan for us, mysterious though it may seem, and we want to be in the center of it.

All the risks notwithstanding, the center of God's will is still the safest place on earth to be.

My soul waits for the Lord
more than the watchmen for the morning.

Psalm 130:6

Acknowledgments

Grateful acknowledgment is made to the following publishers for permission to reprint this copyrighted material. All copyrights are held by the author, Charles R. Swindoll.

The Finishing Touch, (Nashville: Word, 1994).
Laugh Again, (Nashville: Word, 1994).
Hope Again, (Nashville: Word, 1996).
Intimacy with the Almighty, (Nashville: J. Countryman, 1996).
David: A Man of Passion and Destiny, (Nashville: Word, 1997).
Joseph: A Man of Integrity and Forgiveness, (Nashville: Word, 1998).
Esther: A Woman of Strength and Dignity, (Nashville: Word, 1999).
Moses: A Man of Selfless Dedication, (Nashville: Word, 1999).
Perfect Trust, (Nashville: J. Countryman, 2000).
Elijah: A Man of Heroism and Humility, (Nashville: Word, 2000).
Day by Day with Charles Swindoll, (Nashville: Word, 2000).
The Darkness and the Dawn, (Nashville: Word, 2001)
Why, God?, (Nashville: W Publishing Group, 2002).